# DREA DOGZ

# SERVICE DOGS

## INFORMATION EVERY HANDLER
## SHOULD KNOW

## VICTORIA WARFEL
## THERESA A. JENNINGS

For information contact:
Dream Dogz, LLC
Gainesville, Florida
www.DreamK9.com

(352) 278-7404
DreamK9@iCloud.com

Disclaimer: This book is not intended as a substitute for legal advice. If you need legal advice you should seek advice from a qualified attorney. This book is only to be used as an informational source.

For final information on your particular state contact your state's Attorney General's office or Human Rights Commission.

**Dedication**

My interest and true education into laws dealing with Assistance / Service Dogs began with an introduction to the person who later became my mentor in this new world. Kirsten Richards, owner of Service Dog Central website and community forum reinforced the need to read the law as printed from those who made the law. She stressed that it was OK to read blogs, articles and forum discussions on the laws (all opinions of others) but to also go back to the original source to verify. She also instilled in me that when telling others about the law that we needed to let them know that they also needed to read the original and for a final legal decision on matters of importance to their team that they should always go to legal professionals for the final word. It was because of her that I always tried to give a link where anyone interested in learning more through their own research would have a good solid starting point.

The other lady that I would like to dedicate this section to is Victoria Warfel, owner and head trainer of Dream Dogz Behavior Center in Gainesville, FL. Victoria allowed me a location to give workshops in her center and always invited me to set up educational booths on the Assistance Dog Advocacy Project at any community events in which she participated. Victoria has also been a gentle force to keep me going in taking workshop notes and handouts and putting them together into this book. She has also organized the final process of having saleable books ready for the market.

Thank you to both of you ladies in all of your help in this particular travel.

**-Theresa**

Pyro vom Wildhaus
aka "Kaleb"

## Introduction

Throughout the world these dogs working for the disabled are known as Assistance Dogs, but in the United States they are referred to as both Assistance and Service Dogs by organizations and in the laws.

This book has a section of the Florida State Statutes. The section on Federal Law is valuable for all.

Besides the law, this book has information and concepts for all handlers, especially those that decide to owner train with or without professional trainer help.

Boo SD CGC

## Section I

The information in this section is being shared by the Assistance Dog Advocacy Project (ADAP). Unless cited to other sources, the printed material is the work of Theresa A. Jennings, Executive Director of ADAP.

## Some Things to Consider for Owner Training

You need to know the federal and your state's laws. A reputable program should go over these laws with their new handlers. Owner Trainers (OT) will need to take on the responsibility to educate themselves.

While Training:

The ADA, a Federal Civil Rights Law, does not cover Service Dogs In Training (SDIT).

Some states do not cover SDITs while others do.

Some states cover owner training and may give limited rights to the owners, while other states do not acknowledge owner training.

Some states do not acknowledge Psychiatric Service Dogs (PSD) but do acknowledge other Service Dogs (SD). What this means is that if you are training a mobility dog, you can go into places of business, but if you are training a PSD, you can only work in pet-friendly locations.

Some states still do not have a penalty for individuals harassing SDs while working, but as time goes on more states are making this a part of their statutes.

More states are now addressing the issue of those non-disabled people who claim their dogs as SDs.

One of the hardest things in training an Assistance Dog (AD) is picking the correct pup or young dog to work with you for this job. If you do not have experience in selecting working candidates/service dog candidates then you really need the help of someone who does. One of the main reasons an owner trained SD does not make it and needs to be washed from training is because it was not a suitable choice. So it is always advisable to let an expert pick the candidate for you.

A very helpful article to read is:
Elements of Temperament
Drives, Thresholds and Nerves
by Joy Tiz MS, JD

On the training end: Training a SD is not the same as training a pet dog. If someone wants to train their own dog, it is best to do so under the guidance of a reputable and experienced dog trainer with the advanced ability of training a working dog. Just as in the case of owners, not all dog trainers can train a SD in the manner that is needed.

**There are Three Parts to Training a SD:**

1. Obedience

2. Public Access Work

3. Task Training

Warfel's Flying Zola SD CGC TDCH aka "Zoe"
waiting at the airport

## OBEDIENCE

A Service Dog needs more than the basic obedience given to most well-trained pet dogs. If you have never trained a competition or working dog before it would be very beneficial to sign up with a good local pet dog training facility.

Arrow

## PUBLIC ACCESS WORK

Public Access Rights are given to the handler under Title III of the ADA through the Department of Justice (DOJ). The ADA is a Civil Rights Law and as such these rights belong to the disabled handler and not to the trained dog. Legally, this is an important fact to remember.

An interesting read on public access work is given by the International Association of Assistance Dog Partners (IAADP). Please remember that while reading this that it is the standard required by IAADP for its members and is not a requirement of the DOJ.

> *"...a minimum of one hundred twenty (120) hours of schooling over a period of Six Months or more. ... at least thirty (30) hours should be devoted to outings that will prepare the dog to work obediently and unobtrusively in public places."*

The IAADP also requires that a SD be a minimum of 12 months of age.

iaadp.org/iaadp-minimum-training-standards-for-public-access.html

11

## PUBLIC ACCESS TESTING

Owner trainers are more apt to want to find out about these tests since program trained dogs would have already been taken through such a test before being turned over to the new handler. There is no requirement by law that an Assistance Dog must take such a test so we must all remember that it is optional. The ADI PA Test is one that has become greatly recognized in the Service Dog industry. Any trainer may make up their own test form and requirements. We recommend to ask a local trainer if they would be willing to evaluate and sign off on your dog instead of just doing the testing yourself. If the OT does put their dog through such testing it is recommended to keep the handler's copy as part of the paperwork in a training log book.

### Assistance Dogs International (ADI) Public Access Test

Quotes from their test:

> This test was designed to be administered by professional Assistance Dog Trainers.
>
> Assistance Dogs International accepts no responsibility for use of this test.
>
> Copyright Assistance Dogs International, Inc. 1997

A copy of their PA Test can be found on their website. It is available to download at no cost.

assistancedogsinternational.org

## International Association of Assistance Dog Partners (IAADP) on ADI's Testing

Quotes from IAADP Website:

*The Public Access Test evaluates the dog's obedience and manners and the handler's skills in a variety of situations which include:*

*A. The handler's abilities to: ( 1 ) safely load and unload the dog from a vehicle; ( 2 ) enter a public place without losing control of the dog; ( 3 ) to recover the leash if accidentally dropped, and ( 4 ) to cope calmly with an access problem if an employee or customer questions the individual's right to bring a dog into that establishment.*

*B. The dog's ability to: ( 1 ) safely cross a parking lot, halt for traffic, and ignore distractions; ( 2 ) heel through narrow aisles; ( 3 ) hold a Sit-Stay when a shopping cart passes by or when a person stops to chat and pets the dog; (4 ) hold a Down Stay when a child approaches and briefly pets the dog; ( 5 ) hold a*

*Sit Stay when someone drops food on the floor; hold a Down Stay when someone sets a plate of food on the floor within 18" of the dog, then removes it a minute later. [the handler may say "Leave It" to help the dog resist the temptation.] ( 6 ) remain calm if someone else holds the leash while the handler moves 20 ft. away; ( 7 ) remain calm while another dog passes within 6 ft. of the team during the test. This can occur in a parking lot or store. Alternatively, you could arrange for a neighbor with a pet dog to stroll past your residence while you load your dog into a vehicle at the beginning of the test.*

\*\*\* It is highly recommended that the test be video taped to document that the team has passed it.

*IAADP agrees with ADI's ethical position that the amount of training given to an assistance dog should NEVER fall below the minimum level needed to pass this Public Access Test.*

iaadp.org

## TASK TRAINING

The training of tasks is the main part of training that legally defines a dog as a Service Dog under the DOJ. The average time to train a Service Dog is between 18 to 24 months.

M-M Ace SD CGC,
Diabetic Alert Dog (DAD) alerting to low blood glucose

## LOGS

Owner Trainers should keep a very detailed Training Log. If you are ever required to appear in court, the Judge may request you to bring in documentation from your treating doctor that they consider you medically disabled and that in their professional opinion a SD would be of benefit in the treatment plan of your disability. The Judge may also request that training documentation be presented and that you must demonstrate to the Judge what needed tasks your dog has been trained to mitigate your disability. This documentation may also be requested in some housing issues and also in employment.

### Training & Medical Records Log

The log should be some type of a hard cover binder that you can then put topic dividers in. You can put in page protectors for any charts, letters, pictures, outlines and the like.

There are so many ways you can set one up but one idea is:

Topic (Medical) - copies of medical records including copies of medical testing such as OFA hips & elbows, etc.

Topic (Goals) - charts or outlines of training plans such as planned for tasks.

16

Topic (Formal Classwork) - copies of any certificates received from classes taken, letters of praise from instructors, pictures taken during classes.

Topic (Official Certifications) - copies of obedience, behavior, or temperament evaluations such as CGC, ATTS, etc.

Topic (Misc.) - copies of any letters, news articles and such from special events, landlords, veterinary staff, trainers, groomers, etc. that speak of your dog's good manners, training, and behavior. Include any pictures taken of our dog while participating in parades, community fund raising events, posing with mascots such as those at Disney World or sports events.

Topic (Task Training Logs) - charts, etc. showing dates/hours of various task work. Be sure to put down if training goal was met for that particular time or if an unexpected problem came up. If a problem, then write down how you plan to go about correcting the problem.

Topic (Task/Public Access Videos) - taking videos of various stages of training and proofing and then working the dog out in the public are very good ways to document and demonstrate.

Inside of the main top areas, include a method to sub-divide training, proofing, evaluating for the 3 levels: Candidate, In-Training, and Working Levels.

If you ever have need to show documentation of your dog's Public Access training, task training, or proper SD temperament, you have it all together in one easy to locate place.

Axel vom Riverhaus CGC TD aka "Karl"

DREAM DOGZ - SERVICE DOGS

## DOGS FOR SERVICE WORK

### Protection Trained, Breeds or Types of Dogs as Service Dogs

*Alerting to intruders. The phrase "alerting to intruders" is related to the issues of minimal protection and the work or tasks an animal may perform to meet the definition of a service animal. In the original 1991 regulatory text, this phrase was intended to identify service animals that alert individuals who are deaf or hard of hearing to the presence of others. This language has been misinterpreted by some to apply to dogs that are trained specifically to provide aggressive protection, resulting in the assertion that such training qualifies a dog as a service animal under the ADA. The Department reiterates that title II entities are not required to admit any animal whose use poses a direct threat under § 35.139. In addition, the Department has decided to remove the word "intruders" from the service animal definition and replace it with the phrase "the presence of people or sounds." The Department believes this clarifies that so-called "attack training" or other aggressive response types of training that cause a dog to provide an aggressive response do not qualify a dog as a service animal under the ADA.*

*Conversely, if an individual uses a breed of dog that is perceived to be aggressive because of breed reputation, stereotype, or the history or experience the observer*

*may have with other dogs, but the dog is under the control of the individual with a disability and does not exhibit aggressive behavior, the title II entity cannot exclude the individual or the animal from a State or local government program, service, or facility. The animal can only be removed if it engages in the behaviors mentioned in § 35.136(b) (as revised in the final rule) or if the presence of the animal constitutes a fundamental alteration to the nature of the service, program, or activity of the title II entity.*

Also in the same document is this:

*Breed limitations. A few commenters suggested that certain breeds of dogs should not be allowed to be used as service animals. Some suggested that the Department should defer to local laws restricting the breeds of dogs that individuals who reside in a community may own. Other commenters opposed breed restrictions, stating that the breed of a dog does not determine its* propensity for aggression and that aggressive and non-aggressive dogs exist in all breeds.

The Department does not believe that it is either appropriate or consistent with the ADA to defer to local laws that prohibit certain breeds of dogs based on local concerns that these breeds may have a history of unprovoked aggression or attacks. Such deference would have the effect of limiting the rights of persons with disabilities under the ADA who use certain service animals based on where they live rather than on whether the use of a particular animal poses a direct threat to the health and safety of others. Breed restrictions differ significantly from jurisdiction to jurisdiction. Some jurisdictions have no breed restrictions. Others have restrictions that, while well-meaning, have the unintended effect of screening out the very breeds of dogs that have successfully served as service animals for decades without a history of the type of unprovoked aggression or attacks that would pose a direct threat, e.g., German Shepherds. Other jurisdictions prohibit animals over a certain weight, thereby restricting breeds without invoking an express breed ban. In addition, deference to breed restrictions contained in local laws would have the unacceptable consequence of restricting travel by an individual with a disability who uses a *breed that is acceptable and poses no safety hazards in the individual's home jurisdiction but is nonetheless banned by other jurisdictions. Public accommodations have the ability to determine, on a case-by-case basis, whether a particular service animal can be excluded based on that particular animal's actual behavior or history--not based on fears or generalizations about how an animal or breed might behave. This ability to exclude an animal whose behavior or history evidences a direct threat is sufficient to protect health and safety.*

[Federal Register Volume 75, Number 178 (Wednesday, September 15, 2010)]
[Rules and Regulations]
[Pages 56236-56358]
From the Federal Register Online via the Government Printing Office [www.gpo.gov]
[FR Doc No: 2010-21824]

-----------------------------------------------------------------------

DEPARTMENT OF JUSTICE
28 CFR Part 36
[CRT Docket No. 106; AG Order No. 3181-2010]
RIN 1190-AA44
**Nondiscrimination on the Basis of Disability by Public Accommodations and in Commercial Facilities**
AGENCY: Department of Justice, Civil Rights Division.
ACTION: Final rule.

## Size Of Service Dogs

*Size or Weight Limitations. The vast majority of commenters did not support a size or weight limitation. Commenters were typically opposed to a size or weight limit because many tasks performed by service animals require large, strong dogs. For instance, service animals may perform tasks such as providing balance and support or pulling a wheelchair. Small animals may not be suitable for large adults. The weight of the service animal user is often correlated with the size and weight of the service animal. Others were concerned that adding a size and weight limit would further complicate the difficult process of finding an appropriate service animal. One commenter noted that there is no need for a limit because "if, as a practical matter, the size or weight of an individual's service animal creates a direct threat or fundamental alteration to a particular public entity or accommodation, there are provisions that allow for the animal's exclusion or removal." Some common concerns among commenters in support of a size and weight limit were that a larger animal may be less able to fit in various areas with its handler, such as toilet rooms and public seating areas, and that larger animals are more difficult to control.*

*Balancing concerns expressed in favor of and against size and*

*weight limitations, the Department has determined that such limitations would not be appropriate. Many individuals of larger stature require larger dogs. The Department believes it would be inappropriate to deprive these individuals of the option of using a service dog of the size required to provide the physical support and stability these individuals may need to function independently. Since large dogs have always served as service animals, continuing their use should not constitute fundamental alterations or impose undue burdens on public accommodations.*

[Federal Register Volume 75, Number 178 (Wednesday, September 15, 2010)]
[Rules and Regulations]
[Pages 56236-56358]
From the Federal Register Online via the Government Printing Office
[www.gpo.gov]
[FR Doc No: 2010-21824]

---------------------------------------------------------------------

DEPARTMENT OF JUSTICE
28 CFR Part 36
[CRT Docket No. 106; AG Order No. 3181-2010]

RIN 1190-AA44

**Nondiscrimination on the Basis of Disability by Public Accommodations and in Commercial Facilities**

AGENCY: Department of Justice, Civil Rights Division.

ACTION: Final rule.

## TASKS

The views in this section are a culmination of hours of discussions under my SD mentor and friend, Kirsten Richards of Service Dog Central (SDC).

Tasks must be appropriate to the individual and to their disability. All potential owners/ handlers are individuals and each have different needs. The individual should sit down and talk to their medical provider(s) and close friends or family members. These sources can be of great help when deciding what the individual needs. The list should consist of items that the individual needs help with which are things that are necessary for their life functions and they are not able to do on their own or only at a great struggle.

The list for the tasks which legally make a dog a SD should not include items to make the individual feel better emotionally but only to mitigate the person's disability. For the purpose of this list, disregard all emotional feelings and look at the canine partner as a piece of medical equipment versus a warm fuzzy cuddle or something that enhances personal feelings.

Look at the list honestly and decide if a dog is the best choice.

**Tasks are trained.**

The Dept. of Justice has stated that a SD must be "trained tasks" to mitigate the handler's legal disability.

A task is the trained behavior (reaction) to a cue given by the disabled owner.

The following quotes are from Ms. Richards:

> "A task is a trained behavior that mitigates a person's disability by doing something the partner cannot do for themselves, but must be able to do in order to live. Even if you could benefit from a trained behavior, if you could do it for yourself, then it would not qualify as a task for your specific disability. A wheelchair might be a help to a person experiencing stiffness from arthritis, but if they are capable of walking on their own, then a wheelchair isn't really needed. Similarly, a dog trained to remind a handler to take medication, though helpful, would not truly be needed if the person was able to remind themselves to take their medication in ordinary ways, such as using an alarm."

> "To determine how a service dog might help you, make a list of those things you cannot do for yourself because of your disability. Consider what someone might do to help you overcome these barriers to basic functioning. Is it possible a dog might be trained to do those things for you?"

## Strong Tasks and Weak Tasks

Strong Tasks are easily demonstrated.

Weak Tasks are not always easily demonstrated or may be those that are not so clear cut to others, such as a judge in a courtroom setting, as being needed. In some circumstances a weak task may be something the dog is trained to do in very limited circumstances. Example of this last situation may be a dog trained to wake the handler up in the morning but nothing that is needed for a dog being taken out to work in the community during the day. In most cases, a dog waking the handler would be more of a bonus versus a task of any type unless the handler sleeps through alarms etc.

(A bonus is not a true task but something that makes the handler's life easier or more pleasant.)

> In situations where it is not apparent that the dog is a service animal, a business may ask only two questions: 1) is the animal required because of a disability; and 2) what work or task has the animal been trained to perform? No other inquiries about an individual's disability or the dog are permitted. Businesses cannot require proof of certification or medical documentation as a condition for entry.

From the ADA Update: A Primer For Small Business

## How Many Tasks Are Required?

This question is often debated but nowhere in Federal Law is there a clear cut answer. The Dept. of Justice speaks of *tasks* which by itself shows by the plural form that more than one task is required. This is the most direction that they give.

Often quoted is a requirement of 3 tasks minimum. This became the common belief and passed on as part of federal law even though it is not. So where did this "fact" come from? In large part – and probably the main reason – is because of Assistance Dogs International, Inc. (ADI). ADI is a coalition of not for profit organizations that train and place Assistance Dogs. The 3 tasks minimum is part of their Minimum Standards for Training Service Dogs. It is a requirement for organizations that belong to their coalition.

ADI Website http://www.assistancedogsinternational.org

My opinion and speaking as the Founder and Executive Director of ADAP is that any true well-trained Assistance Dog should very easily and reliably be able to do a minimum of 3 strong tasks along with any various weak tasks and bonuses the handler wants to add. Also, as time goes on and the possibility of more judges using this standard in their final decisions this 3 task minimum will likely become more cited in Case Law and thereby may

29

well become a legitimate requirement in future legal decisions.

Boo

Service Dogs are important members of the family.

Ace

## Doing Work Or Performing Tasks

*"Doing work" or "performing tasks." The NPRM proposed that the Department maintain the requirement first articulated in the 1991 title III regulation that in order to qualify as a service animal, the animal must "perform tasks" or "do work" for the individual with a disability. The phrases "perform tasks" and "do work" describe what an animal must do for the benefit of an individual with a disability in order to qualify as a service animal.*

*The Department received a number of comments in response to the NPRM proposal urging the removal of the term "do work" from the definition of a service animal. These commenters argued that the Department should emphasize the performance of tasks instead. The Department disagrees. Although the common definition of work includes the performance of tasks, the definition of work is somewhat broader, encompassing activities that do not appear to involve physical action.*

*One service dog user stated that, in some cases, "critical forms of assistance can't be construed as physical tasks,"* noting that the manifestations of "brain-based disabilities," such as psychiatric disorders and autism, are as varied as their physical counterparts. The Department agrees with this statement but cautions that unless the animal is individually trained to do something that qualifies as work or a task, the animal is a pet or support animal and does not qualify for coverage as a service animal. A pet or support animal may be able to discern that the handler is in distress, but it is what the animal is trained to do in response to this awareness that distinguishes a service animal from an observant pet or support animal.

The NPRM contained an example of "doing work" that stated "a psychiatric service dog can help some individuals with dissociative identity disorder to remain grounded in time or place." 73 FR 34508, 34521 (June 17, 2008). Several commenters objected to the use of this example, arguing that grounding was not a "task" and therefore the example inherently contradicted the basic premise that a service animal must perform a task in order to mitigate a disability. Other commenters stated that "grounding" should not be included as an example of "work" because it could lead to some individuals claiming that they should be able to use emotional support animals in *public because the dog makes them feel calm or safe. By contrast, one commenter with experience in training service animals explained that grounding is a trained task based upon very specific behavioral indicators that can be observed and measured. These tasks are based upon input from mental health practitioners, dog trainers, and individuals with a history of working with psychiatric service dogs.*

*It is the Department's view that an animal that is trained to*

*"ground" a person with a psychiatric disorder does work or performs a task that would qualify it as a service animal as compared to an untrained emotional support animal whose presence affects a person's disability. It is the fact that the animal is trained to respond to the individual's needs that distinguishes an animal as a service animal. The process must have two steps: Recognition and response. For example, if a service animal senses that a person is about to have a psychiatric episode and it is trained to respond, for example, by nudging, barking, or removing the individual to a safe location until the episode subsides, then the animal has indeed performed a task or done work on behalf of the individual with the disability, as opposed to merely sensing an event.*

33

One commenter suggested defining the term "task," presumably to improve the understanding of the types of services performed by an animal that would be sufficient to qualify the animal for coverage. The Department believes that the common definition of the word "task" is sufficiently clear and that it is not necessary to add to the definitions section. However, the Department has added examples of other kinds of work or tasks to help illustrate and provide clarity to the definition. After careful evaluation of this issue, the Department has concluded that the phrases "do work" and "perform tasks" have been effective during the past two decades to illustrate the varied services provided by service animals for the benefit of individuals with all types of disabilities. Thus, the Department declines to depart from its longstanding approach at this time.

*[Federal Register Volume 75, Number 178 (Wednesday, September 15, 2010)]*
*[Rules and Regulations]*
*[Pages 56236-56358]*
*From the Federal Register Online via the Government Printing Office*
*[www.gpo.gov]*
*[FR Doc No: 2010-21824]*

-------------------------------------------------------------------

*DEPARTMENT OF JUSTICE*
*28 CFR Part 36*

*[CRT Docket No. 106; AG Order No. 3181-2010]*

*RIN 1190-AA44*

**Nondiscrimination on the Basis of Disability by Public Accommodations and in Commercial Facilities**

*AGENCY: Department of Justice, Civil Rights Division.*

*ACTION: Final rule.*

## Definitions of Tasks from the Federal Register
*[Federal Register Volume 75, Number 178 (September 15, 2010 )]*
*[Rules and Regulations]*
*[Page 56236-56358]*


DEPARTMENT OF JUSTICE
28 CFR Part 36


## Nondiscrimination on the Basis of Disability by Public Accommodations and in Commercial Facilities

AGENCY: Department of Justice, Civil Rights Division
ACTION: Final regulations
Dated: July 23, 2010
Signed by Attorney General Eric Holder
Effective Date March 15, 2011


Revised definition of "service animal."


*"Service animal means any dog that is individually trained to do work or perform tasks for the benefit of an individual with a disability, including a physical, sensory, psychiatric, intellectual, or other mental disability. Other species of animals, whether wild or domestic, trained or untrained, are not service animals for the purposes of this definition. The work or tasks performed by a service animal must be directly related to the handler's disability. Examples of work or tasks*

*include, but are not limited to, assisting individuals who are blind or have low vision with navigation and other tasks, alerting individuals who are deaf or hard of hearing to the presence of people or sounds, providing non-violent protection or rescue work, pulling a wheelchair, assisting an individual during a seizure, alerting individuals to the presence of allergens, retrieving items such as medicine or the telephone, providing physical support and assistance with balance and stability to individuals with mobility disabilities, and helping persons with psychiatric and neurological disabilities by preventing or interrupting impulsive or destructive behaviors. The crime deterrent effects of an animal's presence and the provision of emotional support, well-being, comfort, or companionship do not constitute work or tasks for the purposes of this definition."*

## ** Corrections or omissions from the following AG Order

*[Federal Register Volume 76, Number 48 (Friday, March 11, 2011)]*
*[Rules and Regulations]*
*[Pages 13286-13288]*
*[FR Doc No: 2011-5581]*

*DEPARTMENT OF JUSTICE*
*28 CFR Part 36*
*[CRT Docket No. 106; AG Order No. 3181-2010]*
*RIN 1190-AA44*

*Nondiscrimination on the Basis of Disability by Public Accommodations and in Commercial Facilities; Corrections*

AGENCY: Department of Justice, Civil Rights Division.

ACTION: Final rule; correction.

Dated: March 7, 2011.

Rosemary Hart,

Special Counsel.

[FR Doc. 2011-5581 Filed 3-10-11; 8:45 am]

BILLING CODE 4410-13-P

SUMMARY:

*This document contains corrections to the final rule published in the Federal Register of Wednesday, September 15, 2010, at 75 FR 56236, relating to nondiscrimination on the basis of disability by public accommodations and in commercial facilities. This document will correct an inadvertent error in an instruction, the omission of some language in the rule, and an error reflected in certain sections of the rule relating to service animals.*

*[[Page 13286 - Page 13287]]*
*Additionally, the final rule contains an error in wording that may cause confusion over the interpretation of the rule. Specifically, on page 56250, in Sec. 36.104*

(``Definitions''), the ``service animal'' definition includes the following language: ``The work or tasks performed by a service animal must be directly related to the handler's disability.'' Because a service animal is not always controlled by the individual with a disability, the service animal's ``handler'' is not necessarily the individual with a disability. To clear up any confusion, the word ``handler's'' should be replaced with the word ``individual's'' in that sentence. Similar use of the word ``handler'' in the section-by-section analysis contained in Appendix A to part 36 also needs to be changed to ``individual'' so it is clear that the individual with a disability does not necessarily need to be the animal's handler in order to be covered by the rule's provisions.

DATES: Effective Date: March 15, 2011.

## Sec. 36.104 [Corrected]

2. On page 56250, in the third column, starting on line 41, in Sec. 36.104, in the definition of ``Service animal'' correct the third sentence of the definition to read as follows: ``The work or tasks performed by a service animal must be directly related to the individual's disability.'

## Appendix A to Part 36 [Corrected]

*4. On page 56266, in the first column, starting on line 15, remove the following sentence: "The work or tasks performed by a service animal must be directly related to the handler's disability" and add in its place the corrected sentence to read as follows: "The work or tasks performed by a service animal must be directly related to the individual's disability."*

*5. On page 56266, in the second column, starting on line 50, remove the following sentence: "Other commenters identified non-violent behavioral tasks that could be construed as minimally protective, such as interrupting self-mutilation, providing safety checks and room searches, reminding the handler to take medications, and protecting the handler from injury resulting from seizures or unconsciousness" and add in its place the corrected sentence to read as follows: "Other commenters identified non-violent behavioral tasks that could be construed as minimally protective, such as interrupting self-mutilation, providing safety checks and room searches, reminding the individual to take medications, and protecting the individual from injury resulting from seizures or unconsciousness."*

*6. On page 56266, in the third column, starting on line 4, remove the sentence that reads: "While many individuals with PTSD may benefit by using a service animal, the work or tasks performed appropriately by* such an animal would not involve unprovoked aggression but could include actively cuing the handler by nudging or pawing the handler to alert to the onset of an episode and removing the individual from the anxiety-provoking environment" and add in its place the corrected sentence to read as follows: "While many individuals with PTSD may benefit by using a service animal, the work or tasks performed appropriately by such an animal would not involve unprovoked aggression, but could include actively cuing the individual by nudging or pawing the individual to alert to the onset of an episode and removing the individual from the anxiety-provoking environment."

7. On page 56267, in the first column, starting on line 40, remove the following sentence: "A pet or support animal may be able to discern that the handler is in distress, but it is what the animal is trained to do in response to this awareness that distinguishes a service animal from an observant pet or support animal" and add in its place the corrected sentence to read as follows: "A pet or support animal may be able to discern that the individual is in distress, but it is what the animal is trained to do in response to this awareness that distinguishes a service animal from an observant pet or support animal."

8. On page 56269, in the second column, starting on line 20, remove the following sentence: ``Tasks performed by psychiatric service animals may include reminding the handler to take medicine, providing safety checks or room searches for persons with PTSD, interrupting self-mutilation, and removing disoriented individuals from dangerous situations" and add in its place the corrected sentence to read as follows: ``Tasks performed by psychiatric service animals may include reminding individuals to take medicine, providing safety checks or room searches for individuals with PTSD, interrupting self-mutilation, and removing disoriented individuals from dangerous situations."

9. On page 56271, in the second column, starting on line 65, remove the following sentence: ``The Department has moved the requirement that the work or tasks performed by the service animal must be related directly to the handler's disability to the definition of `service animal' in Sec. 36.104" and add in its place the corrected sentence to read as follows: ``The Department has moved the requirement that the work or tasks performed by the service animal must be related directly to the individual's disability to the definition of `service animal' in Sec. 36.104."

www.gpo.gov

Karl

## STAGES IN THE LIFE CYCLE OF AN ASSISTANCE/SERVICE DOG

1. Candidate

2. In Training

3. Working Assistance/Service Dog

4. Retired

Under ADAP Guidelines we look at the SDIT Level differently than many. We do a further division and instead of putting a pup or hardly worked with green dog into the SDIT Level we also have a Candidate Level. These dogs are being evaluated to see if they have the temperament and strong health to allow them to flourish as a SDIT.

When a young dog moves up into the SDIT Level we are stating that through testing where available under professional individuals or organizations and our own evaluations of living with these dogs, we are secure that they are ready to be presented as such to the community. We believe that when a dog is taken out into the community as a SDIT that from day one they should be held to a higher standard than that which is acceptable for a pet dog.

We also don't believe in pushing a pup or any dog where it is not ready to go or at a level in which it is not mature enough to flourish. So we have the Candidate Level where we are getting to know our dog and we are watching to see if he is a good choice to continue into the lifestyle path of a potential working dog.

Arrow at Animal Kingdom, Disney World

**Assistance/Service Dog Candidates**

Approximate age – puppy through 12 to 14 months of age

Age based in part on breed and individual dog

Any normal remaining fear imprint stages will be during this time.

Solid housebreaking and basic manners in the home and to pet-friendly locations are part of candidate training.

Puppy and Beginning Obedience training should be completed during this time.

The candidate should continue ongoing health checks and getting age appropriate vet work.

Evaluations on the suitability of the dog should continue.

Foundation work of SD skills and task work can be started at this time. A beginning trick class or reading a book on the subject can be of immense help in laying this foundation.

When working with a pup during the candidate state you need to think and plan on how you will go about working on socialization and habituation. *In speaking of socialization many people tend to meld these two basic concepts into one and label it socialization.*

46

Quote from Kirsten Richards of SDC:

> *Socialization: a systematic introduction of the pup to a wide variety of living creatures, especially different types of people*
>
> *Habituation: a systematic introduction of the pup to a wide variety of things, especially different locations and different surfaces.*

A dog being trained as an Assistance/Service Dog is not a rehab project. If a dog shows people or dog aggression or show shyness or fear when around people acting in a normal manner then the dog should not be elevated from the candidate level.

Until they are fully housebroken, walk nicely on a leash, and show good public manners they should only be going as pets to places where pets are welcomed. It is very important that the candidate not be allowed to form bad habits out in the community at this time.

A candidate should not be dressed in a SDIT cape, wear SDIT patches, nor claimed as a SDIT until ready to be passed up to the SDIT level.

If owner training a young candidate, it is advisable to work the pup to meet the requirements of the AKC S.T.A.R. Puppy.

## Assistance/Service Dogs In Training

Approximate age – 12 to 14 months to 18 to 24 months of age. Age based in part on breed and individual dog

Dogs being used more heavily or as any type of weight bearing dog need to be a full 24 months and only after x-ray evaluation done by a licensed veterinarian.

At this level a dog can begin wearing a SDIT cape, wear SDIT patches, and able to go into the public as such. Trainer needs to know their State Statutes on dogs-in-training, definition on training, and what is required on equipment if there are such in their particular state.

Any dog before going out into the public as a SDIT **should\*** be able to pass the AKC Canine Good Citizen Title or Certification evaluation.

\*Should as is capable of satisfactory completing the 10 tests of the CGC Evaluation - Not that doing the actual evaluation testing is required.

Novice and Advanced Obedience Training should be completed at this time.

Off-leash training and proofing (in a safe location) should be completed.

Dog should be taught/proofed SD skills such as riding on an elevator, going up and down flights of stairs, laying for short amounts of time (such as the time it takes an owner to eat a sandwich and drink) under tables in a restaurant setting if allowed by state statute. If state statute allows then a simple walk through of a grocery store while trainer pushes a cart can be done at this time otherwise continue working in locations that allow pets. Work with dog around automatic doors and past reflective wall surfaces (such as mirrors).

Dogs should be proceeding on basic task training and proofing.

A SDIT should not be dressed in a SD cape, wear SD patches, nor claimed as a SD until ready to be passed up to the SD level.

If possible, it is highly recommend that a dog go through an official. professional type temperament evaluation such as the American Temperament Test (ATTS). http://www.atts.org

Any dog before going out in public as a SD **should\*** be able to pass the AKC Community Canine (CGCA) evaluation and the AKC Urban CGC (CGCU) evaluation.

\*Should as is capable of satisfactory completing the 10 tests of the CGCA and CGCU Evaluation - Not that doing the actual evaluation testing is required.

Any dog before going out into the public as a SD should be able to pass a reputable Public Access Test (PAT) Test designed for SDs.

Before being passed up to SD level advanced health testing (especially those concerns of breed and work of SD) should be completed.

Examples: Orthopedic Foundation for Animals (OFA) Hip & Elbow, Cardiac, Congenital Deafness, Patella Luxation, Thyroid, Tracheal Hypoplasia, Osteochondrosis (OCD) of the shoulder, elbow, stifle, hock, and spine.

For eyes there is the Canine Eye Registry Foundation (CERF).

Some states give owner trainers the same rights as a professional trainer in taking their dog into a non-pet allowed place of business. This right is only to be used while actively training such as taking your dog to a store and having him walk nicely by a cart and going through a check-out line. While training the object is to keep a close eye on the dog and know what needs more work done. This is not the time to take the dog to do your weekly grocery shopping or sitting through a concert. Training sessions are just that — sessions that the owner is teaching and not just passively taking the dog with them out into the public.

**An owner trainer needs to be aware that at any level or stage of training they may have to wash their dog out of training and that their dog may never make it to the**

advanced level that is needed. Emotion, time spent, and money spent on training and having to remove the dog is a risk that is taken by owner training.

Zane, Diabetic Alert Dog in Training,
& Arrow at the movie theater.

## TYPES OF LAWS

Statutory Law: statutes and codes enacted by legislative bodies

Regulatory Law: regulations established by governmental agencies based on statutes

Case Law: rulings (precedents) that can be cited and used in court proceedings

Karl

## FEDERAL LAWS

The United States Code (U.S. Code), a codification of legislation, is the Federal Statutes enacted by Congress (Administrative Law).

Various agencies are mandated by Congress to oversee how the Executive Branch will interpret the U.S. Code. These interpretations or regulations (Regulatory Law) are published in the Codes of Federal Regulation (CFR). To see the annual CFRs go to the U.S. Government Printing Office (GPO) website. www.gpo.gov/fdsys/browse/collectionCfr.action?collectionCode=CFR

From time to time the Supreme Court of the United States (SCOTUS) will make decisions on these interpretations and decide that they are not a reasonable interpretation of the Administrative Law. The Supreme Court has the ultimate authority over Federal Court and any State Court decisions dealing with Federal Law. The mandating Federal Agencies are not able to overthrow the decisions of the Supreme Court – the only way to circumvent the court rulings are to pass a new law as in the case of the ADA and the revised ADA requirements. Members of Congress believed the Supreme Court was not following the original intent of the ADA and through the Amendments reinstated some benefits lost to some persons with disabilities and added or clarified some areas.

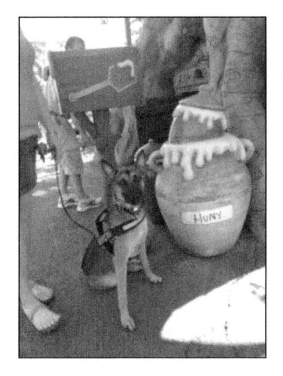

Warfel's Soaring Arrow, SD CGC ITD aka "Arrow" at Magic Kingdom, Disney World

## SERVICE ANIMALS PER THE DEPARTMENT OF JUSTICE AMERICANS WITH DISABILITIES ACT TITLE II PRIMER

U.S. Department of Justice
Civil Rights Division
Disability Rights Section
June 8, 2015

*The ADA does not require service animals to be certified, licensed, or registered as a service animal. Nor are they required to wear service animal vests or patches, or to use a specific type of harness. There are individuals and organizations that sell service animal certification or registration documents to the public. The Department of Justice does not recognize these as proof that the dog is a service animal under the ADA.*

*Under the ADA, a service animal is defined as a dog that has been individually trained to do work or perform tasks for an individual with a disability. The task(s) performed by the dog must be directly related to the person's disability. For example, many people who are blind or have low vision use dogs to guide and assist them with orientation. Many individuals who are deaf use dogs to alert them to sounds. People with mobility disabilities often use dogs to pull their wheelchairs or retrieve items. People with epilepsy may* use a dog to warn them of an imminent seizure, and individuals with psychiatric disabilities may use a dog to remind them to take medication. Dogs can also be trained to detect the onset of a seizure or panic attack and to help the person avoid the attack or be safe during the attack. Under the ADA, "comfort," "therapy," or "emotional support" animals do not meet the definition of a service animal because they have not been trained to do work or perform a specific task related to a person's disability.

Allowing service animals into a "no pet" facility is a common type of reasonable modification necessary to accommodate people who have disabilities. Service animals must be allowed in all areas of a facility where the public is allowed except where the dog's presence would create a legitimate safety risk (e.g., compromise a sterile environment such as a burn treatment unit) or would fundamentally alter the nature of a public entity's services (e.g., allowing a service animal into areas of a zoo where animals that are natural predators or prey of dogs are displayed and the dog's presence would be disruptive). The ADA does not override public health rules that prohibit dogs in swimming pools, but they must be permitted everywhere else.

The ADA requires that service animals be under the control of the handler at all times and be harnessed, leashed, or tethered, unless these devices interfere with the service animal's work or the individual's disability prevents him from using these devices. Individuals who cannot use such devices must maintain control of the animal through voice, signal, or other effective controls.

Public entities may exclude service animals only if 1) the dog is out of control and the handler cannot or does not regain control; or 2) the dog is not housebroken. If a service animal is excluded, the individual must be allowed to enter the facility without the service animal.

Public entities may not require documentation, such as proof that the animal has been certified, trained, or licensed as a service animal, as a condition for entry. In situations where it is not apparent that the dog is a service animal, a public entity may ask only two questions: 1) is the animal required because of a disability? and 2) what work or task has the dog been trained to perform? Public entities may not ask about the nature or extent of an individual's disability.

The ADA does not restrict the breeds of dogs that may be used as service animals. Therefore, a town ordinance that prohibits certain breeds must be modified to allow a person with a disability to use a service animal of a prohibited breed, unless the dog's presence poses a direct threat to the health or safety of others. Public entities have the right to determine, on a *case-by-case basis, whether use of a particular service animal poses a direct threat, based on that animal's actual behavior or history; they may not, however, exclude a service animal based solely on fears or generalizations about how an animal or particular breed might behave.*

ada.gov/regs2010/titleII_2010/title_ii_primer.html#service

Arrow at Epcot, Disney World

## SERVICE ANIMALS ADA REQUIREMENTS
U.S. Department of Justice
Civil Rights Division
Disability Rights Section
ADA 2010 Revised Requirements
July 12, 2011

*The Department of Justice published revised final regulations implementing the Americans with Disabilities Act (ADA) for title II (State and local government services) and title III (public accommodations and commercial facilities) on September 15, 2010, in the Federal Register. These requirements, or rules, clarify and refine issues that have arisen over the past 20 years and contain new, and updated, requirements, including the 2010 Standards for Accessible Design (2010 Standards).*

### Overview

*This publication provides guidance on the term "service animal" and the service animal provisions in the Department's new regulations.*

*Beginning on March 15, 2011, only dogs are recognized as service animals under titles II and III of the ADA.*

*A service animal is a dog that is individually trained to do work or perform tasks for a person with a disability.*

*Generally, title II and title III entities must permit service animals to accompany people with disabilities in all areas where members of the public are allowed to go.*

### How "Service Animal" Is Defined

*Service animals are defined as dogs that are individually trained to do work or perform tasks for people with disabilities. Examples of such work or tasks include guiding people who are blind, alerting people who are deaf, pulling a wheelchair, alerting and protecting a person who is having a seizure, reminding a person with mental illness to take prescribed medications, calming a person with Post Traumatic Stress Disorder (PTSD) during an anxiety attack, or performing other duties. Service animals are working animals, not pets. The work or task a dog has been trained to provide must be directly related to the person's disability. Dogs whose sole function is to provide comfort or* emotional support do not qualify as service animals under the ADA.

This definition does not affect or limit the broader definition of "assistance animal" under the Fair Housing Act or the broader definition of "service animal" under the Air Carrier Access Act.

Some State and local laws also define service animal more broadly than the ADA does. Information about such laws can be obtained from the State attorney general's office.

### Where Service Animals Are Allowed

Under the ADA, State and local governments, businesses, and nonprofit organizations that serve the public generally must allow service animals to accompany people with disabilities in all areas of the facility where the public is normally allowed to go. For example, in a hospital it would be inappropriate to exclude a service animal from areas such as patient rooms, clinics, cafeterias, or examination rooms. However, it may be appropriate to exclude a service animal from operating rooms or burn units where the animal's presence may compromise a sterile environment.

## Service Animals Must Be Under Control

*Under the ADA, service animals must be harnessed, leashed, or tethered, unless these devices interfere with the service animal's work or the individual's disability prevents using these devices. In that case, the individual must maintain control of the animal through voice, signal, or other effective controls.*

## Inquiries, Exclusions, Charges, and Other Specific Rules Related to Service Animals

*When it is not obvious what service an animal provides, only limited inquiries are allowed. Staff may ask two questions: (1) is the dog a service animal required because of a disability, and (2) what work or task has the dog been trained to perform. Staff cannot ask about the person's disability, require medical documentation, require a special identification card or training documentation for the dog, or ask that the dog demonstrate its ability to perform the work or task.*

*Allergies and fear of dogs are not valid reasons for denying access or refusing service to people using service animals. When a person who is allergic to dog dander and a person who uses a service animal must spend time in the same room or* facility, for example, in a school classroom or at a homeless shelter, they both should be accommodated by assigning them, if possible, to different locations within the room or different rooms in the facility.

A person with a disability cannot be asked to remove his service animal from the premises unless: (1) the dog is out of control and the handler does not take effective action to control it or (2) the dog is not housebroken. When there is a legitimate reason to ask that a service animal be removed, staff must offer the person with the disability the opportunity to obtain goods or services without the animal's presence.

Establishments that sell or prepare food must allow service animals in public areas even if state or local health codes prohibit animals on the premises.

People with disabilities who use service animals cannot be isolated from other patrons, treated less favorably than other patrons, or charged fees that are not charged to other patrons without animals. In addition, if a business requires a deposit or fee to be paid by patrons with pets, it must waive the charge for service animals.

If a business such as a hotel normally charges guests for damage that they cause, a customer with a disability may also be charged for damage caused by himself or his service animal.

Staff are not required to provide care or food for a service animal.

## Miniature Horses

In addition to the provisions about service dogs, the Department's revised ADA regulations have a new, separate provision about miniature horses that have been individually trained to do work or perform tasks for people with disabilities. (Miniature horses generally range in height from 24 inches to 34 inches measured to the shoulders and generally weigh between 70 and 100 pounds.) Entities covered by the ADA must modify their policies to permit miniature horses where reasonable. The regulations set out four assessment factors to assist entities in determining whether miniature horses can be accommodated in their facility. The assessment factors are (1) whether the miniature horse is housebroken; (2) whether the miniature horse is under the owner's control; (3) whether the facility can accommodate the miniature horse's type, size, and weight; and (4) whether the miniature horse's presence will not *compromise legitimate safety requirements necessary for safe operation of the facility.*

*For more information about the ADA, please visit our website or call our toll-free number.*

*ADA Website: ADA.gov*

*To receive e-mail notifications when new ADA information is available, visit the ADA Website's home page and click the link near the top of the middle column.*

*ADA Information Line*

*800-514-0301 (Voice) and 800-514-0383 (TTY)*

*24 hours a day to order publications by mail.*

*M-W, F 9:30 a.m. – 5:30 p.m., Th 12:30 p.m. – 5:30 p.m. (Eastern Time) to speak with an ADA Specialist. All calls are confidential.*

*For persons with disabilities, this publication is available in alternate formats.*

*Duplication of this document is encouraged. July 2011*

## FREQUENTLY ASKED QUESTIONS ABOUT SERVICE ANIMALS AND THE ADA

U.S. Department of Justice
Civil Rights Division
Disability Rights Section
July 2015

Many people with disabilities use a service animal in order to fully participate in everyday life. Dogs can be trained to perform many important tasks to assist people with disabilities, such as providing stability for a person who has difficulty walking, picking up items for a person who uses a wheelchair, preventing a child with autism from wandering away, or alerting a person who has hearing loss when someone is approaching from behind.

The Department of Justice continues to receive many questions about how the Americans with Disabilities Act (ADA) applies to service animals. The ADA requires State and local government agencies, businesses, and non-profit organizations (covered entities) that provide goods or services to the public to make "reasonable modifications" in their policies, practices, or procedures when necessary to accommodate people with disabilities. The service animal rules fall under this general principle. Accordingly, entities that have a "no pets" policy generally must modify the policy to allow service animals into their facilities. This publication provides guidance on the ADA's service animal provisions and should be read in conjunction with the publication ADA Revised Requirements: Service Animals.

## DEFINITION OF A SERVICE ANIMAL

Q1. *What is a service animal?*

A. Under the ADA, a service animal is defined as a dog that has been individually trained to do work or perform tasks for an individual with a disability. The task(s) performed by the dog must be directly related to the person's disability.

Q2. *What does "do work or perform tasks" mean?*

A. The dog must be trained to take a specific action when needed to assist the person with a disability. For example, a person with diabetes may have a dog that is trained to alert him when his blood sugar reaches high or low levels. A person with depression may have a dog that is trained to remind her to take her medication. Or, a person who has epilepsy may have a dog that is trained to detect the onset of a seizure and then help the person remain safe during the seizure.

*Q3. Are emotional support, therapy, comfort, or companion animals considered service animals under the ADA?*

A. No. These terms are used to describe animals that provide comfort just by being with a person. Because they have not been trained to perform a specific job or task, they do not qualify as service animals under the ADA. However, some State or local governments have laws that allow people to take emotional support animals into public places. You may check with your State and local government agencies to find out about these laws.

*Q4. If someone's dog calms them when having an anxiety attack, does this qualify it as a service animal?*

A. It depends. The ADA makes a distinction between psychiatric service animals and emotional support animals. If the dog has been trained to sense that an anxiety attack is about to happen and take a specific action to help avoid the attack or lessen its impact, that would qualify as a service animal. However, if the dog's mere presence provides comfort, that would not be considered a service animal under the ADA.

Q5. *Does the ADA require service animals to be professionally trained?*

A. No. People with disabilities have the right to train the dog themselves and are not required to use a professional service dog training program.

Q6. *Are service-animals-in-training considered service animals under the ADA?*

A. No. Under the ADA, the dog must already be trained before it can be taken into public places. However, some State or local laws cover animals that are still in training.

**GENERAL RULES**

Q7. *What questions can a covered entity's employees ask to determine if a dog is a service animal?*

A. In situations where it is not obvious that the dog is a service animal, staff may ask only two specific questions: (1) is the dog a service animal required because of a disability? and (2) what work or task has the dog been trained to perform? Staff are not allowed to request any documentation for the dog, require that the dog demonstrate its task, or inquire about the nature of the person's disability.

Q8. *Do service animals have to wear a vest or patch or special harness identifying them as service animals?*

A. No. The ADA does not require service animals to wear a vest, ID tag, or specific harness.

Q9. *Who is responsible for the care and supervision of a service animal?*

A. The handler is responsible for caring for and supervising the service animal, which includes toileting, feeding, and grooming and veterinary care. Covered entities are not obligated to supervise or otherwise care for a service animal.

Q10. *Can a person bring a service animal with them as they go through a salad bar or other self-service food lines?*

DREAM DOGZ - SERVICE DOGS

A. Yes. Service animals must be allowed to accompany their handlers to and through self-service food lines. Similarly, service animals may not be prohibited from communal food preparation areas, such as are commonly found in shelters or dormitories.

Q11. *Can hotels assign designated rooms for guests with service animals, out of consideration for other guests?*

A. No. A guest with a disability who uses a service animal must be provided the same opportunity to reserve any available room at the hotel as other guests without disabilities. They may not be restricted to "pet-friendly" rooms.

Q12. *Can hotels charge a cleaning fee for guests who have service animals?*

No. Hotels are not permitted to charge guests for cleaning the hair or dander shed by a service animal. However, if a guest's service animal causes damages to a guest room, a hotel is permitted to charge the same fee for damages as charged to other guests.

Q13. *Can people bring more than one service animal into a public place?*

A. Generally, yes. Some people with disabilities may use more than one service animal to perform different tasks. For example, a person who has a visual disability and a seizure disorder may use one service animal to assist with way-finding and another that is trained as a seizure alert dog. Other people may need two service animals for the same task, such as a person who needs two dogs to assist him or her with stability when walking. Staff may ask the two permissible questions (See Question 7) about each of the dogs. If both dogs can be accommodated, both should be allowed in. In some circumstances, however, it may not be possible to accommodate more than one service animal. For example, in a crowded small restaurant, only one dog may be able to fit under the table. The only other place for the second dog would be in the aisle, which would block the space between tables. In this case, staff may request that one of the dogs be left outside.

Q14. *Does a hospital have to allow an in-patient with a disability to keep a service animal in his or her room?*

72

A. Generally, yes. Service animals must be allowed in patient rooms and anywhere else in the hospital the public and patients are allowed to go. They cannot be excluded on the grounds that staff can provide the same services.

Q15. *What happens if a patient who uses a service animal is admitted to the hospital and is unable to care for or supervise their animal?*

A. If the patient is not able to care for the service animal, the patient can make arrangements for a family member or friend to come to the hospital to provide these services, as it is always preferable that the service animal and its handler not be separated, or to keep the dog during the hospitalization. If the patient is unable to care for the dog and is unable to arrange for someone else to care for the dog, the hospital may place the dog in an animal shelter until the patient is released, or make other appropriate arrangements. However, the hospital must give the patient the opportunity to make arrangements for the dog's care before taking such steps.

Q16. *Must a service animal be allowed to ride in an ambulance with its handler?*

A. Generally, yes. However, if the space in the ambulance is crowded and the dog's presence would interfere with the emergency medical staff's ability to treat the patient, staff should make other arrangements to have the dog transported to the hospital.

## CERTIFICATION AND REGISTRATION

Q17. *Does the ADA require that service animals be certified as service animals?*

A. No. Covered entities may not require documentation, such as proof that the animal has been certified, trained, or licensed as a service animal, as a condition for entry.

There are individuals and organizations that sell service animal certification or registration documents online. These documents do not convey any rights under the ADA and the Department of Justice does not recognize them as proof that the dog is a service animal.

Q18. *My city requires all dogs to be vaccinated. Does this apply to my service animal?*

A. Yes. Individuals who have service animals are not exempt from local animal control or public health requirements.

Q19. *My city requires all dogs to be registered and licensed. Does this apply to my service animal?*

A. Yes. Service animals are subject to local dog licensing and registration requirements.

Q20. *My city requires me to register my dog as a service animal. Is this legal under the ADA?*

A. No. Mandatory registration of service animals is not permissible under the ADA. However, as stated above, service animals are subject to the same licensing and vaccination rules that are applied to all dogs.

Q21. *My city / college offers a voluntary registry program for people with disabilities who use service animals and provides a special tag identifying the dogs as service animals. Is this legal under the ADA?*

A. Yes. Colleges and other entities, such as local governments, may offer voluntary registries. Many communities maintain a voluntary registry that

75

serves a public purpose, for example, to ensure that emergency staff know to look for service animals during an emergency evacuation process. Some offer a benefit, such as a reduced dog license fee, for individuals who register their service animals. Registries for purposes like this are permitted under the ADA. An entity may not, however, require that a dog be registered as a service animal as a condition of being permitted in public places. This would be a violation of the ADA.

## BREEDS

Q22. *Can service animals be any breed of dog?*

A. Yes. The ADA does not restrict the type of dog breeds that can be service animals.

Q23. *Can individuals with disabilities be refused access to a facility based solely on the breed of their service animal?*

A. No. A service animal may not be excluded based on assumptions or stereotypes about the animal's breed or how the animal might behave. However, if a particular service animal behaves in a way that poses a direct threat to the health or safety of others, has a history of such behavior, or is not under the control of the handler, that animal may be excluded. If an animal is excluded for such reasons, staff must still offer their goods or services to the person without the animal present.

Q24. *If a municipality has an ordinance that bans certain dog breeds, does the ban apply to service animals?*

A. No. Municipalities that prohibit specific breeds of dogs must make an exception for a service animal of a prohibited breed, unless the dog poses a direct threat to the health or safety of others. Under the "direct threat" provisions of the ADA, local jurisdictions need to determine, on a case-by-case basis, whether a particular service animal can be excluded based on that particular animal's actual behavior or history, but they may not exclude a service animal because of fears or generalizations about how an animal or breed might behave. It is important to note that breed restrictions differ significantly from jurisdiction to jurisdiction. In fact, some jurisdictions have no breed restrictions.

## EXCLUSION OF SERVICE ANIMALS

Q25. *When can service animals be excluded?*

A. The ADA does not require covered entities to modify policies, practices, or procedures if it would "fundamentally alter" the nature of the goods, services, programs, or activities provided to the public. Nor does it overrule legitimate safety requirements. If admitting service animals would fundamentally alter the nature of a service or program, service animals may be prohibited. In addition, if a particular service animal is out of control and the handler does not take effective action to control it, or if it is not housebroken, that animal may be excluded.

Q26. *When might a service dog's presence fundamentally alter the nature of a service or program provided to the public?*

A. In most settings, the presence of a service animal will not result in a fundamental alteration. However, there are some exceptions. For example, at a boarding school, service animals could be restricted from a specific area of a dormitory reserved specifically for students with allergies to dog dander. At a zoo, service animals can be restricted from areas where the animals on display are the natural prey or natural predators of

78

dogs, where the presence of a dog would be disruptive, causing the displayed animals to behave aggressively or become agitated. They cannot be restricted from other areas of the zoo.

Q27. *What does under control mean?  Do service animals have to be on a leash?  Do they have to be quiet and not bark?*

A. The ADA requires that service animals be under the control of the handler at all times. In most instances, the handler will be the individual with a disability or a third party who accompanies the individual with a disability. In the school (K-12) context and in similar settings, the school or similar entity may need to provide some assistance to enable a particular student to handle his or her service animal. The service animal must be harnessed, leashed, or tethered while in public places unless these devices interfere with the service animal's work or the person's disability prevents use of these devices. In that case, the person must use voice, signal, or other effective means to maintain control of the animal. For example, a person who uses a wheelchair may use a long, retractable leash to allow her service animal to pick up or retrieve items. She may not allow the dog to wander away from her and must maintain control of the dog, even if it is retrieving an item at a distance from her. Or, a returning veteran who has PTSD and has great difficulty entering unfamiliar spaces may have a dog that is trained to enter a space, check to see that no threats are there, and come back and signal that it is safe to enter. The dog must be off leash to do its job, but may be leashed at other times. Under control also means that a service animal should not be allowed to bark repeatedly in a lecture hall, theater, library, or other quiet place. However, if a dog barks just once, or barks because someone has provoked it, this would not mean that the dog is out of control.

Q28. *What can my staff do when a service animal is being disruptive?*

A. If a service animal is out of control and the handler does not take effective action to control it, staff may request that the animal be removed from the premises.

Q29. *Are hotel guests allowed to leave their service animals in their hotel room when they leave the hotel?*

A. No, the dog must be under the handler's control at all times.

Q30. *What happens if a person thinks a covered entity's staff has discriminated against him or her?*

A. Individuals who believe that they have been illegally denied access or service because they use service animals may file a complaint with the U.S. Department of Justice. Individuals also have the right to file a private lawsuit in Federal court charging the entity with discrimination under the ADA.

## MISCELLANEOUS

Q31. *Are stores required to allow service animals to be placed in a shopping cart?*

A. No. Generally, the dog must stay on the floor, or the person must carry the dog. For example, if a person with diabetes has a glucose alert dog, he may carry the dog in a chest pack so it can be close to his face to allow the dog to smell his breath to alert him of a change in glucose levels.

Q32. *Are restaurants, bars, and other places that serve food or drink required to allow service* animals to be seated on chairs or allow the animal to be fed at the table?

A. No. Seating, food, and drink are provided for customer use only. The ADA gives a person with a disability the right to be accompanied by his or her service animal, but covered entities are not required to allow an animal to sit or be fed at the table.

Q33. *Are gyms, fitness centers, hotels, or municipalities that have swimming pools required to allow a service animal in the pool with its handler?*

A. No. The ADA does not override public health rules that prohibit dogs in swimming pools. However, service animals must be allowed on the pool deck and in other areas where the public is allowed to go.

Q34. *Are churches, temples, synagogues, mosques, and other places of worship required to allow individuals to bring their service animals into the facility?*

A. No. Religious institutions and organizations are specifically exempt from the ADA. However, there may be State laws that apply to religious organizations.

Q35. *Do apartments, mobile home parks, and other residential properties have to comply with the ADA?*

A. The Fair Housing Act is the Federal law that protects the rights of people with disabilities in residential facilities. For information or to file a complaint, contact the U.S. Department of Housing and Urban Development at 1-800-669-9777.

Q36. *Do Federal agencies, such as the U.S. Department of Veterans Affairs, have to comply with the ADA?*

A. No. Section 504 of the Rehabilitation Act of 1973 is the Federal law that protects the rights of people with disabilities to participate in Federal programs and services. For information or to file a complaint, contact the agency's equal opportunity office.

Q37. *Do commercial airlines have to comply with the ADA?*

A. No. The Air Carrier Access Act is the Federal law that protects the rights of people with disabilities in air travel. For information or to file a complaint, contact the U.S. Department of Transportation, Aviation Consumer Protection Division, at 202-366-2220.

## RESOURCES

For more information about the ADA, please visit our website or call our toll-free number.

### ADA WEBSITE

www.ADA.gov

To receive e-mail notifications when new ADA information is available, visit the ADA Website's home page and click the link near the bottom of the right-hand column.

### ADA INFORMATION LINE

800-514-0301 (Voice) and 800-514-0383 (TTY)

M-W, F 9:30 a.m. – 5:30 p.m. , Th 12:30 p.m. – 5:30 p.m. (Eastern Time) to speak with an ADA Specialist. Calls are confidential.

For people with disabilities, this publication is available in alternate formats.

Duplication of this document is encouraged.

## HEALTH CARE FACILITIES

## Guidelines for Environmental Infection Control in Health-Care Facilities

Recommendations of CDC and the Healthcare Infection Control Practices Advisory Committee (HICPAC)
U.S. Department of Health and Human Services
Centers for Disease Control and Prevention (CDC)
Atlanta, GA 30333
2003

H. Animals in Health-Care Facilities .......................... 105

3. Service Animals ....................................... 108

3. Service Animals

> *Although this section provides an overview about service animals in health-care settings, it cannot address every situation or question that may arise (see Appendix E - Information Resources). A service animal is any animal individually trained to do work or perform tasks for the benefit of a person with a disability. A service animal is not considered a pet but rather an animal trained to provide assistance to a person because of a disability. Title III of the "Americans with Disabilities Act" (ADA) of 1990 mandates that persons with disabilities accompanied by service animals be allowed access with their service*

animals into places of public accommodation, including restaurants, public transportation, schools, and health-care facilities. In health-care facilities, a person with a disability requiring a service animal may be an employee, a visitor, or a patient.

An overview of the subject of service animals and their presence in health-care facilities has been published. No evidence suggests that animals pose a more significant risk of transmitting infection than people; therefore, service animals should not be excluded from such areas, unless an individual patient's situation or a particular animal poses greater risk that cannot be mitigated through reasonable measures. If health-care personnel, visitors, and patients are permitted to enter care areas (e.g., inpatient rooms, some ICUs, and public areas) without taking additional precautions to prevent transmission of infectious agents (e.g., donning gloves, gowns, or masks), a clean, healthy, well behaved service animal should be allowed access with its handler. Similarly, if immunocompromised patients are able to receive visitors without using protective garments or equipment, an exclusion of service animals from this area would not be justified.

*Because health-care facilities are covered by the ADA or the Rehabilitation Act, a person with a disability may be accompanied by a service animal within the facility unless the animal's presence or behavior creates a fundamental alteration in the nature of a facility's services in a particular area or a direct threat to other persons in a particular area. A "direct threat" is defined as a significant risk to the health or safety of others that cannot be mitigated or eliminated by modifying policies, practices, or procedures. The determination that a service animal poses a direct threat in any particular healthcare setting must be based on an individualized assessment of the service animal, the patient, and the health-care situation. When evaluating risk in such situations, health-care personnel should consider the nature of the risk (including duration and severity); the probability that injury will occur; and whether reasonable modifications of policies, practices, or procedures will mitigate the risk (J. Wodatch, U.S. Department of Justice, 2000). The person with a disability should contribute to the risk-assessment process as part of a pre-procedure health-care provider/ patient conference.*

*Excluding a service animal from an OR or similar special care areas (e.g., burn units, some ICUs, PE units, and any other area containing equipment critical for life support) is appropriate if these areas are considered to have "restricted access" with regards to the general public. General infection-control measures that dictate such limited access include a) the area is required to meet environmental criteria to minimize the risk of disease transmission, b) strict attention to hand hygiene and absence of dermatologic conditions, and c) barrier protective measures [e.g., using gloves, wearing gowns and masks] are indicated for persons in the affected space. No infection-control measures regarding the use of barrier precautions could be reasonably imposed on the service animal. Excluding a service animal that becomes threatening because of a perceived danger to its handler during treatment also is appropriate; however, exclusion of such an animal must be based on the actual behavior of the particular animal, not on speculation about how the animal might behave.*

*Another issue regarding service animals is whether to permit persons with disabilities to be accompanied by their service animals during all phases of their stay in the health-care facility.*

*Healthcare personnel should discuss all aspects of anticipatory care with the patient who uses a service animal.*

*Health-care personnel may not exclude a service animal because health-care staff may be able to perform the same services that the service animal does (e.g., retrieving dropped items and guiding an otherwise ambulatory person to the restroom). Similarly, health-care personnel can not exclude service animals because the health-care staff perceive a lack of need for the service animal during the person's stay in the health-care facility. A person with a disability is entitled to independent access (i.e., to be accompanied by a service animal unless the animal poses a direct threat or a fundamental alteration in the nature of services); "need" for the animal is not a valid factor in either analysis. For some forms of care (e.g., ambulation as physical therapy following total hip replacement or knee replacement), the*

*service animal should not be used in place of a credentialed health-care worker who directly provides therapy. However, service animals need not be restricted from being in the presence of its handler during this time; in addition, rehabilitation and discharge planning should incorporate the patient's future use of the animal. The health-care* personnel and the patient with a disability should discuss both the possible need for the service animal to be separated from its handler for a period of time during nonemergency care and an alternate plan of care for the service animal in the event the patient is unable or unwilling to provide that care. This plan might include family members taking the animal out of the facility several times a day for exercise and elimination, the animal staying with relatives, or boarding off-site. Care of the service animal, however, remains the obligation of the person with the disability, not the health-care staff.

Although animals potentially carry zoonotic pathogens transmissible to man, the risk is minimal with a healthy, clean, vaccinated, well-behaved, and well-trained service animal, the most common of which are dogs and cats. No reports have been published regarding infectious disease that affects humans originating in service dogs. Standard cleaning procedures are sufficient following occupation of an area by a service animal. Clean-up of spills of animal urine, feces, or other body substances can be accomplished with blood/body substance procedures outlined in the Environmental Services section of this guideline. No special bathing procedures are required prior *to a service animal accompanying its handler into a health-care facility.*

*Providing access to exotic animals (e.g., reptiles and non-human primates) that are used as service animals is problematic. Concerns about these animals are discussed in two published reviews.Because some of these animals exhibit high-risk behaviors that may increase the potential for zoonotic disease transmission (e.g., herpes B infection), providing health-care facility access to nonhuman primates used as service animals is discouraged, especially if these animals might come into contact with the general public. Health-care administrators should consult the Americans with Disabilities Act for guidance when developing policies about service animals in their facilities.*

*Requiring documentation for access of a service animal to an area generally accessible to the public*

*would impose a burden on a person with a disability. When health-care workers are not certain that an animal is a service animal, they may ask the person who has the animal if it is a service animal required because of a disability; however, no certification or other documentation of service animal status can be required.*

cdc.gov/hicpac/pdf/guidelines/eic_in_HCF_03.pdf

## HOUSING

### Service Animal or Emotional Support Animal -- Dog or Other in Housing Issues

Most housing issues are under the Dept. of Housing and Urban Development (HUD). While the DOJ only considers dog's that are *trained* to mitigate (tasks and work) for their disabled handler to fit in their Regulations, HUD uses a broader range of animals (including other domestic animals) to fit into theirs.

Another important point that may cause confusion is that while the DOJ only allows two questions to be asked by a business in Public Access, HUD allows a landlord to go into more depth when reviewing a Request for Reasonable Accommodation. If a person's disability is not readily apparent a landlord may request a letter or form signed by the medical provider who is treating the owner in which it is stated that the dog (or other animal) is providing some type of service to the owner's disability.

Also , the DOJ (Articles II and III) require that the dog is trained to mitigate the handler's disability while HUD's position is "that animals necessary as a reasonable accommodation do not necessarily need to have specialized training. Some animals perform tasks that require training, and others provide assistance that does not require training."

See more info in Federal Register on Monday, October 27, 2008

24 CFR Part 5

Pet Ownership for the Elderly and Persons With Disabilities;

Final Rule

In a Request for Reasonable Accommodation, a dog can be excluded based on breed or type of dog if the landlord can show that by accepting this particular it would be an undue burden in regards to insurance purposes. In other words that their insurance would greatly increase or that it would in fact be dropped.

For more on this you may want to read the Memo that addresses this issue titled Insurance Policy Restrictions dated June 12, 2006.

When reading Regulations and other documents it is helpful to keep in mind that some agencies use the term *Service* while others use *Assistance* or at times both may be used.

Arrow at the doctor office.

# JOINT STATEMENT OF THE DEPARTMENT OF HOUSING AND URBAN DEVELOPMENT AND THE DEPARTMENT OF JUSTICE

## REASONABLE ACCOMMODATIONS UNDER THE FAIR HOUSING ACT

Washington, D.C.
May 17, 2004

Introduction

> The Department of Justice ("DOJ") and the Department of Housing and Urban Development ("HUD") are jointly responsible for enforcing the federal Fair Housing Act1 (the "Act"), which prohibits discrimination in housing on the basis of race, color, religion, sex, national origin, familial status, and disability.*2 One type of disability discrimination prohibited by the Act is the refusal to make reasonable accommodations in rules, policies, practices, or services when such accommodations may be necessary to afford a person with a disability the equal opportunity to use and enjoy a dwelling.*3

94

*HUD and DOJ frequently respond to complaints alleging that housing providers have violated the Act by refusing reasonable accommodations to persons with disabilities. This Statement provides technical assistance regarding the rights and obligations of persons with disabilities and housing providers under the Act relating to\*4 Housing providers that receive federal financial assistance are also subject to the requirements of Section 504 of the Rehabilitation Act of l973.*

*The Act prohibits housing providers from discriminating against applicants or residents because of their disability or the disability of anyone associated with them\*5 and from treating persons with disabilities less favorably than others because of their disability. The Act also makes it unlawful for any person to refuse "to make reasonable accommodations in rules, policies, practices, or services, when such accommodations may be necessary to afford... person(s) [with disabilities] equal opportunity to use and enjoy a dwelling."\*6*

*[Under the Examples Section - Under Question 6]*
*Example 3: A housing provider has a "no pets" policy. A tenant who is deaf requests that the provider allow him to keep a dog in his unit as a*

*reasonable accommodation. The tenant explains that the dog is an assistance animal that will alert him to several sounds, including knocks at the door, sounding of the smoke detector, the telephone ringing, and cars coming into the driveway. The housing provider must make an exception to its "no pets" policy to accommodate this tenant.*

*[Under Question 11}*
*Example 2: Because of his disability, an applicant with a hearing impairment needs to keep an assistance animal in his unit as a reasonable accommodation. The housing provider may not require the applicant to pay a fee or a security deposit as a condition of allowing the applicant to keep the assistance animal. However, if a tenant's assistance animal causes damage to the applicant's unit or the common areas of the dwelling, the housing provider may charge the tenant for the cost of repairing the damage (or deduct it from the standard security deposit imposed on all tenants), if it is the provider's practice to assess tenants for any damage they cause to the premises.*

*[Under Question 17]*
*Example 2: A rental applicant who uses a*

*wheelchair advises a housing provider that he wishes to keep an assistance dog in his unit even though the provider has a "no pets" policy. The applicant's disability is readily apparent but the need for an assistance animal is not obvious to the provider. The housing provider may ask the applicant to provide information about the disability-related need for the dog.*

*When a person with a disability believes that she has been subjected to a discriminatory housing practice, including a provider's wrongful denial of a request for reasonable accommodation, she may file a complaint with HUD within one year after the alleged denial or may file a lawsuit in federal district court within two years of the alleged denial. If a complaint is filed with HUD, HUD will investigate the complaint at no cost to the person with a disability.*

*There are several ways that a person may file a complaint with HUD:*

*• By placing a toll-free call to 1-800-669-9777 or TTY 1-800-927-9275;*

*• By completing the "on-line" complaint form available on the HUD internet site:*

*http://www.hud.gov; or*

• *By mailing a completed complaint form or letter to:*

*Office of Fair Housing and Equal Opportunity*
*Department of Housing & Urban Development*
*451 Seventh Street, S.W., Room 5204*
*Washington, DC 20410-2000*

*The Civil Rights Division of the Justice Department brings lawsuits in federal courts across the country to end discriminatory practices and to seek monetary and other relief for individuals whose rights under the Fair Housing Act have been violated. The Civil Rights Division initiates lawsuits when it has reason to believe that a person or entity is involved in a "pattern or practice" of discrimination or when there has been a denial of rights to a group of persons that raises an issue of general public importance. The Division also participates as amicus curiae in federal court cases that raise important legal questions involving the application and/or interpretation of the Act. To alert the Justice Department to matters involving a pattern or practice of discrimination, matters involving the denial of rights to groups of persons, or lawsuits raising issues that may be appropriate for amicus participation, contact:*

*U.S. Department of Justice*
*Civil Rights Division*
*Housing and Civil Enforcement Section – G St.*
*950 Pennsylvania Avenue, N.W.*
*Washington, DC 20530*

*1. The Fair Housing Act is codified at 42 U.S.C. §§ 3601 - 3619.*

*2. The Act uses the term "handicap" instead of the term "disability." Both terms have the*

*same legal meaning. See Bragdon v. Abbott, 524 U.S. 624, 631 (1998) (noting that definition of*

*"disability" in the Americans with Disabilities Act is drawn almost verbatim "from the definition*

*of 'handicap' contained in the Fair Housing Amendments Act of 1988"). This document uses the*

*term "disability," which is more generally accepted.*

*3. 42 U.S.C. § 3604(f)(3)(B).*

*4. 29 U.S.C. § 794. Section 504, and its implementing regulations at 24 C.F.R. Part 8, prohibit discrimination based on disability and require recipients of federal financial assistance to provide reasonable accommodations to applicants and residents with disabilities. Although Section 504 imposes greater obligations than the Fair Housing Act, (e.g., providing and paying for reasonable accommodations that involve structural modifications to units or public and common areas), the principles discussed in this Statement regarding reasonable accommodation under the Fair Housing Act generally apply to requests for reasonable accommodations to rules, policies, practices, and services under Section 504. See U.S. Department of Housing and Urban Development, Office of Public and Indian Housing, Notice PIH 2002-01(HA) (www.hud.gov/offices/fheo/disabilities/ PIH02-01.pdf) and "Section 504: Frequently Asked Questions," (www.hud.gov/offices/fheo/ disabilities/sect504faq.cfm#anchor272118).*

*5. The Fair Housing Act's protection against disability discrimination covers not only home seekers with disabilities but also buyers and renters without disabilities who live or are associated with individuals with disabilities 42 U.S.C. § 3604(f)(1) (B), 42 U.S.C. § 3604(f)(1)(C), 42 U.S.C. § 3604(f)(2)(B), 42 U.S.C. § (f)(2)(C). See also H.R. Rep. 100-711 – 24 (reprinted in 1988 U.S.C.A.N. 2173, 2184-85) ("The Committee intends these provisions to prohibit not only discrimination against the primary purchaser or named lessee, but also to prohibit denials of housing opportunities to applicants because they have children, parents, friends, spouses, roommates, patients, subtenants or other associates who have disabilities.")*. *Accord: Preamble to Proposed HUD Rules Implementing the Fair Housing Act, 53 Fed. Reg. 45001 (Nov. 7, 1988) (citing House Report).*

*6. 42 U.S.C. § 3604(f)(3)(B). HUD regulations pertaining to reasonable accommodations may be found at 24 C.F.R. § 100.204.*

Arrow at a store

US DEPARTMENT OF HOUSING AND URBAN DEVELOPMENT

Office of Fair Housing and Equal Opportunity

Washington, DC 20410-2000

June 12, 2006

Memorandum for: FHEO Regional Directors

From: Bryan Greene, Deputy Assistant Secretary for Enforcement and Programs, ED

Subject: **Insurance Policy Restrictions as a Defense for Refusals to Make a Reasonable Accommodation**

> *This memorandum responds to requests for guidance on how HUD investigators should examine Fair Housing Act "reasonable accommodation" cases where a housing provider cites an insurance policy restriction in denying a request form a person with a disability to reside in a dwelling with an assistance animal that is of a breed of dog that the landlord's insurance carrier considers dangerous. In the referenced cases, the housing providers stated that their insurance carriers will either refuse to cover their properties, substantially increase the cost of coverage, or*

*adversely change the terms of their policies if these animals are allowed to occupy dwellings.*

*As with any request for a reasonable accommodation, the request should be evaluated on a case-by-case basis. HUD provides the following guidance to assist in that evaluation.*

*According to the Joint Statement on Reasonable Accommodations, an accommodation is unreasonable if it imposes an undue financial and administrative burden on a housing provider's operations. If a housing provider's insurance carrier would cancel, substantially increase the costs of the insurance policy, or adversely change the policy terms because of the presence of a certain breed of dog or a certain animal, HUD will find that this imposes an undue financial and administrative burden on the housing provider. However, the investigator must substantiate the coverage, by verifying such a claim with the insurance company directly and considering whether comparable insurance, without the restriction, is available in the market. If the investigator finds evidence that an insurance provider has a policy of refusing to insure any housing that has animals, without exception for assistance animals, it may refer that information to the Department of Justice for investigation to* determine whereto the insurance provider has violated federal civil rights laws prohibiting discrimination based upon disability.

## Department of Housing and Urban Development (HUD)

Congress mandated different sections "Articles" to be overseen by various federal agencies. One of those agencies is HUD. As printed in the Federal Register / Vol. 73, No. 208 / Monday, October 27, 2008 / Rules and Regulations is a ruling on when to allow animals in a no-pet housing situation. This ruling addresses the topic of Emotional Support Animals.

DEPARTMENT OF HOUSING AND URBAN DEVELOPMENT
24 CFR Part 5
[Docket No. FR–5127–F–02]
RIN 2501–AD31

## Pet Ownership for the Elderly and Persons With Disabilities

AGENCY: Office of the Secretary, HUD.
ACTION: Final rule.
SUMMARY:

*This final rule amends HUD's regulations governing the requirements for pet ownership in HUD-assisted public housing and multifamily housing projects for the elderly and persons with disabilities. Specifically, this final rule conforms these pet ownership requirements to the requirements for animals assisting persons with disabilities in HUD's public housing programs, other than housing projects for the elderly or persons with disabilities. This final rule follows publication of an October 15, 2007, proposed rule, and takes into consideration the public comments received on the proposed rule. In response to one comment, HUD has made a nonsubstantive change to the proposed rule. Specifically, consistent with the phrasing used in HUD's public housing pet ownership regulations, this final rule amends the assisted housing regulations to refer to "animals that assist, support, or provide service to persons with disabilities."*

*DATES: Effective Date: November 26, 2008.*

hud.gov/offices/fheo/FINALRULE/
Pet_Ownership_Final_Rule.pdf

Some highlights (direct quotes) from this ruling:

*The prescribed pet rules place reasonable limitations on pet ownership to ensure the health, safety, and well-being of all residents.*

*Under both the Fair Housing Act and Section 504, in order for a requested accommodation to qualify as a reasonable accommodation, the requester must have a disability, and the accommodation must be necessary to afford a person with a disability an equal opportunity to use and enjoy a dwelling.*

*The Department's position has been that animals necessary as a reasonable accommodation do not necessarily need to have specialized training. Some animals perform tasks that require training, and others provide assistance that does not require training.*

*Housing providers are entitled to verify the existence of the disability, and the need for the accommodation — if either is not readily apparent. Accordingly, persons who are seeking a reasonable accommodation for an emotional support animal may be required to provide documentation from a physician, psychiatrist, social worker, or other mental health professional that the animal provides support that alleviates at least one of the identified symptoms or effects of the existing disability.*

*In addition, housing providers are not required to provide any reasonable accommodation that would pose a direct threat to the health or safety of others.*

*Moreover, a housing provider is not required to make a reasonable accommodation if the presence of the assistance animal would (1) result in substantial physical damage to the property of others unless the threat can be eliminated or significantly reduced by a reasonable accommodation; (2) pose an undue financial and administrative burden; or (3) fundamentally alter the nature of the provider's operations.*

*Emotional support animals by their very nature, and without training, may relieve depression and anxiety,* and/or help reduce stress-induced pain in persons with certain medical conditions affected by stress.

The Department does not agree that the definition of the term "service animal" contained in the Department of Justice regulations implementing the ADA should be applied to the Fair Housing Act and Section 504. The ADA governs the use of animals by persons with disabilities primarily in the public arena. There are many areas where the ADA and the Fair Housing Act and Section 504 contain different requirements.

The following notice was sent from John Trasvina, Assistant Secretary for Fair Housing and Equal Opportunity. In it is noted that the definition of a service animal is broader than that given by the DOJ in Titles II and III. Animals other than dogs can be considered service animals in addition to all known as Emotional Support Animals (ESA) under U.S. Dept. of HUD when dealing with certain housing issues. As printed here the notice is not complete and only shows some of the highlights. To read in full go to: portal.hud.gov/hudportal/documents/huddoc? id=servanimals_ntcfheo2013-01.pdf

U.S. DEPARTMENT OF HOUSING AND URBAN DEVELOPMENT
WASHINGTON. DC 20410-2000
SPECIAL ATTENTION OF:
HUD Regional and Field Office Directors of Public and Indian
Housing (PIH);
Housing; Community Planning and Development (CPD),
Fair Housing and Equal Opportunity; and Regional Counsel;
CPD, P11-1 and Housing Program Providers
FHEO Notice: **FHEO-2013-01**
Issued: April 25, 2013
Expires: Effective until
Amended, Superseded, or Rescinded


Subject: **Service Animals and Assistance Animals for People with Disabilities in Housing and HUD-Funded Programs**

*Purpose: This notice explains certain obligations of housing providers under the Fair Housing Act (FHAct), Section 504 of the Rehabilitation Act of 1973 (Section 504), and the Americans with Disabilities Act (ADA) with respect to animals that provide assistance to individuals with disabilities. The Department of Justice's (DOT) amendments to its regulations' for Titles II and III of the ADA limit the definition of "service animal" under the ADA to include only dogs, and further define "service animal" to exclude emotional support animals. This definition, however, does not limit housing providers' obligations to make*

109

DREAM DOGZ - SERVICE DOGS

*reasonable accommodations for assistance animals under the FHAct or Section 504. Persons with disabilities may request a reasonable accommodation for any assistance animal, including an emotional support animal, under both the FHAct and Section 504. In situations where the ADA and the FHAct/ Section 504 apply simultaneously (e.g., a public housing agency, sales or leasing offices, or housing associated with a university or other place of education), housing providers must meet their obligations under both the reasonable accommodation standard of the FHAct/Section 504 and the service animal provisions of the ADA.*

*Applicability: This notice applies to all housing providers covered by the FHAct, Section 504, and/or the ADA\*2. 2Title II of the ADA applies to public entities, including public entities that provide housing, e.g., public housing agencies and state and local government provided housing, including housing at state universities and other places of education. In the housing context. Title III of the ADA applies to public accommodations, such as rental offices, shelters, some types of multifamily housing, assisted living facilities and housing at places of public education. Section 504 covers housing providers that receive federal financial assistance from the U.S. Department of Housing and Urban Development (HUD). The Fair Housing Act covers virtually all types of housing, including privately* owned housing and federally assisted housing, with a few limited exceptions.

An assistance animal is not a pet. It is an animal that works, provides assistance, or performs tasks for the benefit of a person with a disability, or provides emotional support that alleviates one or more identified symptoms or effects of a person's disability. Assistance animals perform many disability-related functions, including but not limited to, guiding individuals who are blind or have low vision, alerting individuals who are deaf or hard of hearing to sounds, providing protection or rescue assistance, pulling a wheelchair, fetching items, alerting persons to impending seizures, or providing emotional support to persons with disabilities who have a disability-related need for such support. For purposes of reasonable accommodation requests, neither the FHAct nor Section 504 requires an assistance animal to be individually trained or certified.*5. While dogs are the most common type of assistance animal, other animals can also be assistance animals. 5For a more detailed discussion on assistance animals and the issue of training, see the preamble to HUD's final rule, Pet Ownership for the elderly and Persons With Disabilities, 73 Fed. Reg. 63834,63835 (October 27, 2008).

The request may also be denied if: (1) the specific assistance animal in question poses a direct threat to the health or safety of others that cannot be reduced or eliminated by another reasonable accommodation, or (2) the specific assistance animal in question would cause substantial physical damage to the property of others that cannot be reduced or eliminated by another reasonable accommodation. Breed, size, and weight limitations may not be applied to an assistance animal.

Housing providers may ask individuals who have disabilities that are not readily apparent or known to the provider to submit reliable documentation of a disability and their disability-related need for an assistance animal. If the disability is readily apparent or known but the disability-related need for the assistance animal is not, the housing provider may ask the individual to provide documentation of the disability related need for an assistance animal.

Certain entities will be subject to both the service animal requirements of the ADA and the reasonable accommodation provisions of the FHAct and/or Section 504. These entities include, but are not limited to, public housing agencies and some places of public accommodation, such as rental offices, shelters, residential homes, some types of multifamily housing, assisted living facilities, and housing at places of education.

DREAM DOGZ - SERVICE DOGS

*If the animal does not meet the ADA service animal test, then the housing provider must evaluate the request in accordance with the guidance provided in Section I of this notice.*

*It is the housing provider's responsibility to know the applicable laws and comply with each of them.*

*Conclusion*

*The definition of "service animal" contained in ADA regulations does not limit housing providers' obligations to grant reasonable accommodation requests for assistance animals in housing under either the FHAct or Section 504. Under these laws, rules, policies, or practices must be modified to permit the use of an assistance animal as a reasonable accommodation in housing when its use may be necessary to afford a person with a disability an equal opportunity to use and enjoy a dwelling and/or the common areas of a dwelling, or may be necessary to allow a qualified individual with a disability to participate in, or benefit from, any housing program or activity receiving financial assistance from HUD.*

**TRAVEL**

**Air Travel**

For problems at the airport, ask for the Complaint Resolution Official (CRO) be called. A CRO is required to be on duty at the airport when the airport is operational.

**The Air Carrier Access Act (ACAA)**
Department of Transportation (DOT)

§ 382.37 Seat assignments.

> (c) If a service animal cannot be accommodated at the seat location of the qualified individual with a disability whom the animal is accompanying (see § 382.55(a)(2)), the carrier shall offer the passenger the opportunity to move with the animal to a seat location, if present on the aircraft, where the animal can be accommodated, as an alternative to requiring that the animal travel with checked baggage.

§ 382.38 Seating accommodations.

> For an individual traveling with a service animal, the carrier shall provide, as the individual requests,

*either a bulkhead seat or a seat other than a bulkhead seat.*

## § 382.55 Miscellaneous provisions.

*Carriers shall permit dogs and other service animals used by persons with a disability to accompany the persons on a flight.*

*Carriers shall accept as evidence that an animal is a service animal identification cards, other written documentation, presence of harnesses or markings on harnesses, tags, or the credible verbal assurances of the qualified individual with a disability using the animal.*

*Carriers shall permit a service animal to accompany a qualified individual with a disability in any seat in which the person sits, unless the animal obstructs an aisle or other area that must remain unobstructed in order to facilitate an emergency evacuation.*

*In the event that special information concerning the transportation of animals outside the continental United States is either required to be or is provided by the carrier, the information shall be provided to all passengers traveling with animals outside the continental United States with the carrier, including those traveling with service animals.*

Discrimination Complaints

Complaints may be sent to:

Aviation Consumer Protection Division

Attn: C-75-D

U.S. Department of Transportation

400 7th Street, S.W. Washington, D.C. 20590

OR

airconsumer@ost.dot.gov

Arrow at the airport

## GUIDANCE CONCERNING SERVICE ANIMALS

From Nondiscrimination on the Basis of Disability in Air Travel 73 FR 27614, May 13, 2008, as modified by:

• Correction Notice of 74 FR 11469, March 18, 2009

• Correction Notice of 75 FR 44885, July 30, 2010

This document includes the modifications from both Correction Notices.

DEPARTMENT OF TRANSPORTATION

14 CFR Part 382

[Dockets OST–2004–19482; OST–2005–22298; OST–2006–23999]

[RINs 2105–AC97; 2105–AC29; 2105–AD41]

## Nondiscrimination on the Basis of Disability in Air Travel

AGENCY: Department of Transportation, Office of the Secretary

ACTION: Final Rule

EFFECTIVE DATE: This rule is effective May 13, 2009.

## Introduction

*In 1990, the U.S. Department of Transportation (DOT) promulgated the official regulations implementing the Air Carrier Access Act (ACAA). Those rules are entitled Nondiscrimination on the Basis of Disability in Air Travel (14 CFR Part 382). Since then the number of people with disabilities*

117

*traveling by air has grown steadily. This growth has increased the demand for air transportation accessible to all people with disabilities and the importance of understanding DOT's regulations and how to apply them. This document expands on an earlier DOT guidance document published in 19963, which was based on an earlier Americans with Disabilities Act (ADA) service animal guide issued by the Department of Justice (DOJ) in July 1996. The purpose of this document is to aid airline employees and people with disabilities in understanding and applying the ACAA and the provisions of Part 382 with respect to service animals in determining:*

*(1) whether an animal is a service animal and its user a qualified individual with a disability;*

*(2) how to accommodate a qualified person with a disability with a service animal in the aircraft cabin; and*

*(3) when a service animal legally can be refused carriage in the cabin.*

*This guidance will also be used by Department of Transportation staff in reviewing the implementation of §382.117 of this Part by carriers.*

## Background

*The 1996 DOT guidance document defines a service animal as "any guide dog, signal dog, or other animal individually trained to provide assistance to an individual with a disability. If the animal meets this definition, it is considered a service animal regardless of whether it has been licensed or certified by a state or local government." This document refines DOT's previous definition of service animal by making it clear that animals that assist persons with disabilities by providing emotional support qualify as service animals and ensuring that, in situations concerning emotional support animals and psychiatric service animals, the authority of airline personnel to require documentation of the individual's disability and the medical necessity of the passenger traveling with the animal is understood.*

## Two Steps for Airline Personnel

*To determine whether an animal is a service animal and should be allowed to accompany its user in the cabin, airline personnel should:*

*1. Establish whether the animal is a pet or a service animal, and whether the passenger is a qualified individual with a disability; and then*

*2. Determine if the service animal presents either a "direct threat to the health or safety of others," or a significant threat of disruption to the airline service in the cabin (i.e., a "fundamental alteration" to passenger service). See §382.19(c).*

## Service Animals

*How do I know it's a service animal and not a pet?*

*Remember: In most situations the key is TRAINING. Generally, a service animal is individually trained to perform functions to assist the passenger who is a qualified individual with a disability. In a few extremely limited situations, an animal such as a seizure alert animal may be capable of performing functions to assist a qualified person with a disability without individualized training. Also, an animal used for emotional support need not have specific training for that function. Similar to an animal that has been individually trained, the definition of a service animal includes: an animal that has been shown to have the innate ability to assist a person with a disability; or an emotional support animal.*

*These five steps can help one determine whether an animal is a service animal or a pet:*

*1. Obtain credible verbal assurances: Ask the passenger: "Is this your pet?" If the passenger responds that the animal is a service animal and not a pet, but uncertainty remains about the animal, appropriate follow-up questions would include:*

*"What tasks or functions does your animal perform for you?" or*

*"What has it been trained to do for you?"*

*"Would you describe how the animal performs this task (or function) for you?"*

*As noted earlier, functions include, but are not limited to:*

*A. helping blind or visually impaired people to safely negotiate their surroundings;*

*B. alerting deaf and hard-of-hearing persons to sounds;*

*C. helping people with mobility impairments to open and close doors, retrieve objects, transfer from one seat to another, maintain balance; or*

D. alert or respond to a disability-related need or emergency (e.g., seizure, extreme social anxiety or panic attack).

Note that to be a service animal that can properly travel in the cabin, the animal need not necessarily perform a function for the passenger during the flight. For example, some dogs are trained to help pull a passenger's wheelchair or carry items that the passenger cannot readily carry while using his or her wheelchair. It would not be appropriate to deny transportation in the cabin to such a dog.

If a passenger cannot provide credible assurances that an animal has been individually trained or is able to perform some task or function to assist the passenger with his or her disability, the animal might not be a service animal. In this case, the airline personnel may require documentation (see Documentation below).

There may be cases in which a passenger with a disability has personally trained an animal to perform a specific function (e.g., seizure alert). Such an animal may not have been trained through a formal training program (e.g., a "school" for service animals). If the passenger can provide a reasonable explanation of how the animal was trained or how it performs the function for which it is being used, this can constitute a "credible verbal *assurance"* that the animal has been trained to perform a function for the passenger.

*2. Look for physical indicators on the animal: Some service animals wear harnesses, vests, capes or backpacks. Markings on these items or on the animal's tags may identify it as a service animal. It should be noted, however, that the absence of such equipment does not necessarily mean the animal is not a service animal. Similarly, the presence of a harness or vest on a pet for which the passenger cannot provide such credible verbal assurance may not be sufficient evidence that the animal is, in fact, a legitimate service animal.*

*3. Request documentation for service animals other than emotional support or psychiatric service animals: The law allows airline personnel to ask for documentation as a means of verifying that the animal is a service animal, but DOT's rules tell carriers not to require documentation as a condition for permitting an individual to travel with his or her service animal in the cabin unless a passenger's verbal assurance is not credible. In that case, the airline may require documentation as a condition for allowing the animal to travel in the cabin. This should be an infrequent situation. The purpose of documentation is to substantiate the passenger's disability-related need for the animal's*

123

accompaniment, which the airline may require as a condition to permit the animal to travel in the cabin. Examples of documentation include a letter from a licensed professional treating the passenger's condition (e.g., physician, mental health professional, vocational case manager, etc.)

4. Require documentation for emotional support and psychiatric service animals: With respect to an animal used for emotional support (which need not have specific training for that function but must be trained to behave appropriately in a public setting), airline personnel may require current documentation (i.e., not more than one year old) on letterhead from a licensed mental health professional, including a medical doctor that is treating the passenger's mental or emotional disability stating (1) that the passenger has a mental health-related disability listed in the Diagnostic and Statistical Manual of Mental Disorders (DSM IV); (2)that having the animal accompany the passenger is necessary to the passenger's mental health or treatment; (3) that the individual providing the assessment of the passenger is a licensed mental health professional and the passenger is under his or her professional care; and (4) the date and type of the mental health professional's license and the state or other

jurisdiction in which it was issued. Airline personnel may require this documentation as a condition of permitting the animal to accompany the passenger in the cabin. The purpose of this provision is to prevent abuse by passengers that do not have a medical need for an emotional support

animal and to ensure that passengers who have a legitimate need for emotional support animals are permitted to travel with their service animals on the aircraft. Airlines are not permitted to require the documentation to specify the type of mental health disability, e.g., panic attacks.

There is a separate category of service animals generally known as "psychiatric service animals." These animals may be trained by their owners, sometimes with the assistance of a professional trainer, to perform tasks such as fetching medications, reminding the user to take medications, helping people with balance problems caused by medications or an underlying condition, bringing a phone to the user in an emergency or activating a specially equipped emergency phone, or acting as a buffer against other people crowding too close). As with emotional support animals, it is possible for this category of animals to be a source of abuse by persons attempting to circumvent carrier rules concerning transportation of pets. Consequently, it is appropriate for airlines to apply the same advance notice and documentation requirements to psychiatric service animals as they do to emotional support animals.

5. Observe behavior of animals: Service animals are trained to behave properly in public settings. For example, a properly trained guide dog will remain at its owner's feet. It does not run freely around an aircraft or an airport gate area, bark or growl repeatedly at other persons on the aircraft, bite or jump on people, or urinate or defecate in the cabin or gate area. An animal that engages in such disruptive behavior shows that it has not been successfully trained to function as a service animal in public settings. Therefore, airlines are not required to treat it as a service animal, even if the animal performs an assistive function for a passenger with a disability or is necessary for a passenger's emotional well-being.

**What about service animals in training?**

Part 382 requires airlines to allow service animals to accompany their handlers in the cabin of the aircraft, but airlines are not required otherwise to carry animals of any kind either in the cabin or in

126

the cargo hold. Airlines are free to adopt any policy they choose regarding the carriage of pets and other animals (e.g., search and rescue dogs) provided that they comply with other applicable requirements (e.g., the Animal Welfare Act). Although "service animals in training" are not pets, the ACAA does not include them, because "in training" status indicates that they do not yet meet the legal definition of service animal.

However, like pet policies, airline policies regarding service animals in training vary. Some airlines permit qualified trainers to bring service animals in training aboard an aircraft for training purposes. Trainers of service animals should consult with airlines, and become familiar with their policies.

What about a service animal that is not accompanying a qualified individual with a disability?

When a service animal is not accompanying a passenger with a disability, the airline's general policies on the carriage of animals usually apply. Airline personnel should know their company's policies on pets, service animals in training, and the carriage of animals generally. Individuals planning to travel with a service animal other than

127

*their own should inquire about the applicable policies in advance.*

*Further Notes:*

*Service animal users typically refer to the person who accompanies the animal as the "handler."*

*The above are parts of a larger document. To read in full go to the link given below.*

airconsumer.ost.dot.gov/rules/Part%20382-2008.pdf

Arrow taking a break at
Magic Kingdom, Disney World

## TSA CARES

Planning on Flying with your SD? Have questions about screening policies? Want to know what to expect at a security checkpoint?

Latest revision: 27 June 2014

Call TSA Cares toll-free at 1-855-787-2227, Monday through Friday 8 a.m. – 11 p.m. EST, and weekends and holidays 9 a.m. – 8 p.m. EST.

www.tsa.gov

## Traveling with Special Items -- SERVICE ANIMAL

*** If you have a service animal, please tell the TSA officer that the animal with you is a service animal and not a pet. This way you can move to the front of the screening line since the TSA officer may need to spend more time with you.*

*** We recommend that you carry verification that your animal is a service animal. This may include: cards or documentation, presence of a harness or markings on the harness, or other credible verification.*

*** You will not be separated from your service animal during the screening process.*

129

** *TSA officers have been trained not to communicate, distract, interact, play, feed, or pet service animals.*

** *The TSA officer should ask permission before touching your service animal or its belongings.*

** *Please control your service animal while the TSA officer conducts the inspection. You are required to ensure the animal cannot harm the TSA officer.*

** *If you need to leave the secure boarding area to relieve your animal, you must undergo the full screening process again. When you return to the security checkpoint, tell the TSA officer you are back and she/he will move you to the front of the screening line.*

www.tsa.gov/traveler-information/service-animals


## SERVICE DOGS

** *Tell the TSA officer the best way for you and your dog to go through the metal detector as a team (i.e., whether walking together or with the service dog walking in front of or behind you).*

** *If the metal detector alarms when you and your service dog walk through together, both you and the dog must undergo additional screening.*

\** *If the metal detector alarms on either you or your service dog individually (because you walked through separately), whoever set off the alarm must have additional screening.*

\** *If your service dog alarms the walk-through metal detector, the TSA officer will ask for your permission and help before touching your service dog and its belongings. The TSA officer will then perform a physical inspection of your dog and its belongings (collar, harness, leash, backpack, vest, etc.) The TSA officer will not remove your dog's belongings.*

## ANSWERS TO FREQUENTLY ASKED QUESTIONS CONCERNING AIR TRAVEL OF PEOPLE WITH DISABILITIES

### Under the Amended Air Carrier Access Act Regulation

UNITED STATES OF AMERICA
DEPARTMENT OF TRANSPORTATION
OFFICE OF AVIATION ENFORCEMENT AND PROCEEDINGS
WASHINGTON, DC
May 13, 2009

Issued on 05/13/09 by the Office of the Assistant General Counsel for Aviation Enforcement and Proceedings and its Aviation Consumer Protection Division.

Information from this document dealing with Service Dogs:

**Section 382.11 (a)(3) – Non-discrimination and Benefits of Air Transportation Related Services**

> *5. If a carrier's premium service includes airline-provided transportation from the customer's home or a central pick-up location in the city to the airport, must that transportation be accessible to passengers with disabilities?*

*Answer: Yes. Both U.S. and foreign air carriers are subject to ACAA requirements generally prohibiting discrimination in the provision of air transportation and related services (14 CFR 382.11(a)(1) and (3)). If an airline provides ground transportation services to its premium customers (e.g., first class passengers or elite frequent flyers), the Aviation Enforcement Office would regard the failure or refusal of an airline to provide "equivalent service" to a passenger with a disability in connection with a covered flight in the same class of service as a violation of these provisions.*

*382.27 – Advance Notice*

*10. When must a carrier accommodate a passenger accompanied by an emotional support or psychiatric service animal who has not provided 48 hours' advance notice?*

*Answer: Carriers must accommodate a passenger accompanied by an emotional support or psychiatric service animal who has not provided 48 hours' advance notice if the carrier can do so by making reasonable efforts, without delaying a flight. The carrier, at its discretion, may waive its 48 hours' advance notice requirement in order to expedite the short-notice air travel of a passenger* accompanied by an emotional support or psychiatric service animal.

*16. Where should carriers and airports establish the service animal relief areas required at U.S. airports under the rule?*

*Answer: While not specifically required by our rule, carriers and airports may wish to consider the benefits of establishing animal relief areas both inside and outside the secure area (e.g., to accommodate passengers with short connection times, to minimize time needed for escort service, passenger convenience). In doing so, carriers should consult with service animal training organizations. In establishing animal relief areas inside the secure area, carriers and airports should coordinate closely with the Transportation Security Administration (TSA) and the Customs and Border Protection (CBP) offices serving the airport to ensure that the animal relief area can be used consistent with TSA and CBP procedures.*

*17. Who is responsible for the installation and maintenance of service animal relief areas at U.S. airports?*

*Answer: Animal relief areas should be provided in cooperation between airlines and the airport operator and in consultation with local service animal training organization(s).*

*20. How will travelers accompanied by assistance dogs/service animals know where the relief areas are located in U.S. airports?*

*Answer: Passengers who request that the carrier provide them with assistance to an animal relief area should be advised by the carrier of the location of the animal relief area. Additionally, if requested, it would be the responsibility of the carrier to accompany a passenger traveling with a service animal to and from the animal relief area. The requirement to provide animal relief areas is effective on May 13, 2009, for U.S. carriers and May 13, 2010, for foreign carriers.*

## Section 382.81 – Seating Accommodations

*24. Can an airline require passengers with a disability accompanied by service animals to sit in the bulkhead row?*

135

*Answer: No. As stated in 382.81 (c), a passenger with a disability traveling with a service animal must be provided, as the passenger requests, either a bulkhead seat or a seat other than a bulkhead seat that would accommodate the service animal subject to applicable safety regulations. If the passenger chooses a seat other than a bulkhead seat, the carrier is not required to permit the passenger to specify a particular seat of his or her choosing (e.g., "7C") that he or she would not be entitled to under the carrier's normal seat-selection procedures, except to the extent necessary to accommodate the animal as required by sections 382.117(b) and (c) of the rule.*

*25. May a carrier exclude a passenger with a disability seeking to travel with a service animal from his or her specific assigned seat or require that passenger to sit in a particular seat in the cabin?*

*Answer: No, except to comply with FAA or applicable foreign government safety regulations. A service animal may be placed at the feet of a person with a disability at any bulkhead seat or in any other seat as long as when the animal is seated/placed/curled up on the floor, no part of the animal extends into the main aisle(s) of the* aircraft and the service animal is not at an emergency exit row seat.

29. Who is responsible for providing escort assistance to an airport service animal relief area and how can a passenger accompanied by a service animal obtain such assistance?

Answer: Airlines are responsible for providing assistance to animal relief areas upon request at those airports where such animal relief areas are required. Airlines are free to use contractors to provide this service. Passengers can obtain such assistance by requesting it from appropriate airline personnel. (See question 20 also dealing with service animal relief escort assistance.)

## Section 382.117 – Service Animals

33. What type of documentation are carriers permitted to require as a condition of permitting a service animal to travel on a flight segment scheduled to take 8 hours or more?

Answer: The carrier may require documentation that the animal will not need to relieve itself during the expected duration of the flight or that the animal can relieve itself in a way that does not

137

create a health or sanitation issue on the flight. Examples of documentation a passenger could provide include either a written statement from a veterinarian, a signed statement from the passenger containing the procedures that he/she employs to prevent the animal from having to relieve itself (e.g., limitation on the provision of food and water) and an assurance that the use of these procedures has prevented the animal from relieving itself for a period similar to that of the planned duration of the flight, or a signed statement with photographs or other illustrations of the animal's ability to relieve itself without posing a health or sanitation problem (e.g., the use of a passenger-provided absorbent plastic-backed pad).

34. May carriers require documentation that an animal accompanying a passenger with a disability is a service animal?

Answer: Generally no, except in limited circumstances as discussed below. Unless a foreign carrier has received a conflict of laws waiver permitting the carrier to impose such a requirement, or the carrier finds that the verbal assurances of the passenger are not credible and there are no other indications of the animal's status such as a harness, tag or vest, the airline may not

138

require such documentation. Carriers are permitted to require documentation for emotional support animals and psychiatric service animals.

35. What conditions may carriers impose on the transport of service dogs?

Answer: Carriers must transport all service dogs (e.g., guide dogs, seizure alert dogs, etc.) as long as safety and animal health requirements are met.

36. Must carriers accept emotional support and psychiatric support animals in the aircraft cabin?

Answer: U.S. carriers must accept any emotional support or psychiatric service animal in the aircraft cabin consistent with applicable safety and animal health requirements and ensure that its foreign code share partners do the same on covered flights with respect to passengers traveling under the U.S. carrier's code. Foreign carriers must accept any emotional support or psychiatric service dog in the aircraft cabin consistent with applicable safety and animal health requirements on covered flights.

37. What should airline personnel do if a passenger with a disability is accompanied in the

airplane cabin by a service animal that does not fit in the space immediately in front of the passenger and there is no other seat in the cabin with sufficient space to safely accommodate the animal?

Answer: If a service animal does not fit in the space immediately in front of the accompanying passenger with a disability and there is no other seat with sufficient space to safely accommodate the animal and its partner (i.e., user), there are several options to consider for accommodating the service animal in the cabin in the same class of service. The carrier should speak with other passengers to find a passenger in an adjacent seat who is willing to share foot space with the animal, or a passenger in a seat adjacent to a location where the service animal can be accommodated (e.g., in the space behind the last row of seats) or adjacent to an empty seat, who is willing to exchange seats with the service animal's partner. As noted in the preamble to our rule, there are probably no circumstances in which the purchase of a second seat would be necessary to accommodate the service animal. If a class of service on a flight is totally filled, there would not be any seat available for purchase. If the class of service had even one middle seat unoccupied, *the passenger with a service animal could be seated next to the vacant seat. It is likely that even a large animal (e.g., Great Dane) could use some of the floor space of the vacant seat, making any further purchase by the passenger unnecessary. Only if there is no alternative available to enable the passenger to travel with the service animal in the cabin on that flight should the carrier offer options such as transporting the service animal in the cargo hold or transportation on a later flight with more room. When transportation on a later flight is offered, carriers are strongly encouraged, but not required by Part 382, to allow any passenger who wishes to rebook on a different flight to the same destination and on the same airline to do so at the same fare.*

*38. If a carrier determines that a service animal cannot accompany a passenger with a disability in the cabin due to a behavior problem on the part of the animal that may result in a direct threat to the health or safety of others or a fundamental alteration in service, what should the carrier do?*

*Answer: The carrier should first permit the passenger to try available means of mitigating the problem (e.g., muzzling a barking service dog) before deciding to exclude the service animal from* the cabin. If those means are not successful, the carrier may follow its company policy on pets because the animal has shown that it has not been successfully trained to function as a service animal in public settings. Whenever the airline decides not to accept an animal for travel as a service animal, the airline must provide the passenger a written explanation of its decision within 10 calendar days of the incident.

39. If a carrier determines that a service animal cannot accompany a disabled passenger in the cabin and the passenger refuses to allow the animal to be transported in the cargo hold and requests instead to be rebooked on a later flight, must the carrier do so without additional charge?

Answer: If an airline cannot safely transport a service animal (e.g., because it is too large to fit anywhere in the cabin), a carrier must follow its nondiscriminatory contract of carriage provisions applicable to the passenger's fare in determining how to best reaccommodate such passengers. Although not required by Part 382, carriers are strongly encouraged to allow any such passengers who wish to rebook on a different flight to the same destination and on the same airline to do so at the same fare.

*40. How can a passenger accompanied by a service animal find out whether the country he or she is traveling to has animal health regulations that carriers as well as the passenger with a service animal must comply with in order to ensure the legal entry of the service animal into that country?*

*Answer: Passengers should always confirm well in advance with the embassy or consulate of the country they plan to visit and with the airline on which they will be traveling, which animal health regulations apply. Most countries have animal health regulations that require certain health conditions to be met before an animal can be legally admitted to the country. At a minimum, most countries require a valid rabies vaccination certificate issued by a licensed veterinarian. Additional health measures may be required within specified time frames before you travel and species restrictions may also apply. Passengers should be aware that many islands have similar restrictions, even for animals traveling from the mainland of the same country (e.g., Hawaii), and check with the island's designated animal health authority before traveling to determine what conditions apply.*

*41. For purposes of providing documentation stating a passenger's disability-related need for an emotional support or psychiatric service animal, what kind of practitioners qualify as "licensed mental health professionals"?*

*Answer: Any licensed mental health professional (e.g., psychiatrist, psychologist, licensed clinical social worker) including a medical doctor who is specifically treating a passenger's mental or emotional disability is a practitioner qualified to provide documentation stating the passenger's need for an emotional support or psychiatric service animal. A qualified practitioner would include a general practitioner who is treating the passenger's mental or emotional disability.*

*42. May a carrier require that the documentation a passenger provides in order to travel with an animal that is used as an emotional support or psychiatric service animal state the passenger's specific mental or emotional condition?*

*Answer: No. A carrier may only require that a passenger's documentation confirm that a passenger has a mental or emotional disability recognized in the Diagnostic and Statistical Manual of Mental Disorders- Fourth Edition (DSM-*

*IV), in addition to three other items (i.e., the passenger needs the animal for air travel and/or activity at the passenger's destination, the individual providing the assessment is a licensed mental health professional and that passenger is under his/her care, the date and type of mental health professional's license and the state or other jurisdiction in which it was issued).*

*43. May a carrier accept documentation from a licensed mental health professional concerning a passenger's need for a psychiatric or emotional support animal if the documentation is more than one year old?*

*Answer: Carriers may, at their discretion, accept from the passenger with a disability documentation from his or her licensed mental health professional that is more than one year old. We encourage carriers to consider accepting "outdated" documentation in situations where such passenger provides a letter or notice of cancellation or other written communication indicating the cessation of health insurance coverage, and his/her inability to afford treatment for his or her mental or emotional disability.*

## Section 382.121 – Stowage of Mobility Aids and Other Assistive Devices in the Cabin

*44. When may a bag containing an assistive device be counted towards a passenger's carry-on bag limit?*

*Answer: An assistive device is any piece of equipment that assists a passenger with a disability to hear, see, communicate, maneuver, or perform other functions of daily life, and may include medical devices and medications.*

## Section 382.125 - Assistive Devices Stowed in the Cargo Compartment

*47. Are food and equipment that a service animal requires to function as a service animal considered assistive devices under Part 382?*

*Answer: Equipment used by a service animal (e.g., harness, leash, vest) in conjunction with its work as a service animal is an assistive device under the rule. Food is not equipment under this definition and therefore when tendered as carry-on or checked baggage, the standard size, weight, and baggage allowance limits of the carrier may apply.*

airconsumer.ost.dot.gov/rules/FAQ_5_13_09.pdf

*********************

Some airlines will allow any gear including food for a Service Dog to be considered as allowable under Assistive Device and will not charge for this bag to be flown. All items must be for the dog only. Check with your airline when booking your flight for their updated information.

If traveling by air keep the following info where you can get to it easily:

If you have any problems at the airport ask for the Complaint Resolution Office to be notified at once. The CRO must be available whenever the airport is open.

## AMTRAK

From their webpage:

### Service Animals

*Generally, animals are not allowed on Amtrak. However, service animals are permitted in all areas where passengers are allowed. Service animals are animals that are trained to perform a specific task for the benefit of a person with a disability. Amtrak personnel may ask what task(s) the service animal performs. Carry-on pet guidelines do not pertain to passengers traveling with service animals.*

### Making Reservations with Service Animals

*It is not possible to make reservations that include service animals on Amtrak.com. Amtrak encourages passengers using service animals to make reservations by phone so that we can reserve an accessible seat or space (if desired) and provide you with information regarding intermediate station stops. Call 1-800-USA-RAIL (1-800-872-7245) or TTY (1-800-523-6590). Agents are available 24 hours a day, 7 days a week.*

*For more info visit their Service Animal and Pet Policy at amtrak.com/service-animals-and-pet-policy*

M-M Hero, Diabetic Alert Dog (DAD) in Training indicating low glucose.

## TAXICABS, SHUTTLES AND LIMOUSINE SERVICES

The above may not deny services even if they hold a no pet policy. They may not require advance notice or any type of paperwork. The company may not charge higher fees or any additional charge for cleaning over any that they charge a passenger traveling without a SD. As in any public access situation the SD must be under control at all times and must be housebroken.

Further information on this topic may be found through the Department of Justice or by calling toll-free the ADA Information Line at 800-514-0301 (voice) or 800-514-0383 (TDD).

## ACCESSIBLE LODGING

### Places of Public Lodging

The Department of Justice (DOJ) has issued revised ADA regulations under Title III, which cover many types of private businesses, or "places of public accommodation." Many of these revisions apply to Places of Lodging such as new requirements for reservation systems, and revised and new standards for facility access [28 C.F.R. §§ 36.104, 36.302(e), 36.406(c)].

Definition: What is a "Place of Lodging?"

Places of lodging include:
hotels
motels
inns
other facilities that offer sleeping rooms for short-term stays (generally 30 days or less) and that meet certain conditions (for more information see ADA Title III Regulations, Section 36.104).

### Staying in Hotels

*People with disabilities who use service animals cannot be isolated from other patrons, treated less favorably than other patrons, or charged fees that are not charged to other patrons without animals.*

*In addition, if a business requires a deposit or fee to be paid by patrons with pets, it must waive the charge for service animals.*

ADA Business BRIEF: Service Animals

ada.gov/svcanimb.htm

\*\*\*\*\*\*\*\*\*\*

*If a business such as a hotel normally charges guests for damage that they cause, a customer with a disability may also be charged for damage caused by himself or his service animal.*

*Staff are not required to provide care or food for a service animal.*

Revised ADA Regulations: Service Animals

ada.gov/service_animals_2010.htm

## DEPARTMENT OF THE INTERIOR

### National Parks Service (NPS)

*The U.S. Department of the Interior has control over the National Parks Service. The NPS is legally required to allow Service Dogs into the national parks system per Section 504 of the Rehabilitation Act and use the definition given by the DOJ within 28CFR36.104 and as such are not considered to be pets nor required to follow any pet regulations within the NPS. There are times and locations that may have restrictions in allowing a SD into the area based on safety of people, wildlife and the SDs themselves. SDs should be kept on leash, unless verified with a Park Ranger that it is OK to turn them loose for exercise.*

*It is recommended before visiting any park to find out what their restrictions are. More information on the NPS can be found at nps.gov/index.htm*

## SECTION 504 OF THE REHAB ACT

People with disabilities as defined in section 705(20) of this title can not be discriminated against for benefits under the following:

• Federal Executive Agencies

• Programs and Activities receiving Federal Financial Assistance

• U.S. Postal Service

• Some Federal Buildings

Exempted from this Act are:

• Federal Courts -- It is up to the individual Judge if he will allow a SD into his courtroom

• The White House

• U.S. Congress

154

The Rehab Act was the first U.S. Federal Civil Rights Law for the protection of people with disabilities. It later was the base from which other current Civil Rights Laws began including the ADA. Many people still believe that the ADA is the law of the land, but this is not true. Congress mandated a great number of areas to be under various Federal Agencies when passing the ADA but not all. When discussing access issues with their Service Dog, people often cite the ADA as their source of being allowed onto USPS property where in truth it is the Rehab Act they should reference.

## U.S. POSTAL SERVICES (USPS)
ELECTRONIC CODE OF FEDERAL REGULATIONS
Title 39 → Chapter I → Subchapter D → Part 232 → §232.1

Title 39: Postal Service
PART 232—CONDUCT ON POSTAL PROPERTY

*§232.1 Conduct on postal property.*

*(a) Applicability. This section applies to all real property under the charge and control of the Postal Service, to all tenant agencies, and to all persons entering in or on such property. This section shall be posted and kept posted at a conspicuous place on all such property.*

*(5)(j) Dogs and other animals. Dogs and other animals, except those used to assist persons with disabilities, must not be brought upon postal property for other than official purposes.*

Warfel's Jedi Knight during public access training.

## AMERICAN DISABILITIES ACT (ADA)

### The ADA of 1990 and ADAAA of 2008

The Americans with Disabilities Act (ADA) and the revised Americans with Disabilities Act Amendments Act of 2008 (ADAAA) also known as the ADA Amendments Act of 2008 are both Civil Rights Laws passed by Congress.

### The Americans with Disabilities Act of 1990 (ADA)

An Act to establish a clear and comprehensive prohibition of discrimination on the basis of disability. Be it enacted by the Senate and House of Representatives of the United States of America assembled, that this Act may be cited as the "Americans with Disabilities Act of 1990".

### ADA Amendments Act of 2008 (ADAAA)

On September 25, 2008, President George W. Bush signed into law the ADA Amendments Act of 2008.

The Final Regulations were signed by Attorney General Eric Holder July 23, 2010

The ADA Amendments Act of 2008 (ADAAA) was printed in the Federal Register on September 15, 2010, and effective on March 15, 2011.

## TITLE I (EMPLOYMENT)

EEOC www.eeoc.gov/facts/performance-conduct.html

Title I of the Americans with Disabilities Act (ADA) and Section 501 of the Rehabilitation Act, which prohibit employment discrimination against qualified individuals with disabilities, generally do not impinge on the right of employers to define jobs and to evaluate their employees according to consistently applied standards governing performance and conduct. Under both laws, employees with disabilities must meet qualification standards that are job-related and consistent with business necessity and must be able to perform the "essential functions" of the position, with or without reasonable accommodation.

Title I of the ADA covers private, state, and local government employers with 15 or more employees; Section 501 of the Rehabilitation Act of 1973 covers federal agencies. The statutes contain identical anti-discrimination provisions.

An employee with a disability must meet the same production standards, whether quantitative or qualitative, as a non-disabled employee in the same job. Lowering or changing a production standard because an employee cannot meet it due to a disability is not considered a reasonable accommodation. However, a reasonable accommodation may be required to assist an employee in meeting a specific production standard.

The Department of Justice published revised final regulations implementing the Americans with Disabilities Act (ADA) for title II (State and local government services) and title III (public accommodations and commercial facilities) on September 15, 2010, in the Federal Register. These requirements, or rules, clarify and refine issues that have arisen over the past 20 years and contain new, and updated, requirements, including the 2010 Standards for Accessible Design (2010 Standards).

Department of Justice (DOJ) www.ada.gov

> *"Generally, title II and title III entities must permit service animals to accompany people with disabilities in all areas where members of the public are allowed to go."*

~ U.S. Department of Justice Civil Rights Division Disability Rights Section

## TITLE II (PUBLIC ENTITIES)

The Department of Justice's regulation implementing title II, subtitle A, of the ADA which prohibits discrimination on the basis of disability in all services, programs, and activities provided to the public by State and local governments, except public transportation services.

*Document below is not in full. Only sections of greater interest to Service Dog Handlers has been copied.*

Federal Register, The Daily Journal of the United States Government
**Nondiscrimination on the Basis of Disability in State and Local Government Services**
A Rule by the Justice Department on 09-15-2010

ACTION: Final Rule.

SUMMARY:

*This final rule revises the regulation of the Department of Justice (Department) that implements title II of the Americans with Disabilities Act (ADA), relating to nondiscrimination on the basis of disability in State and local government services. The Department is issuing this final rule in order to adopt enforceable accessibility standards under the ADA that are consistent with the minimum guidelines and requirements issued by the Architectural and Transportation Barriers Compliance Board (Access Board), and to update or amend certain provisions of the title II regulation so that they comport with the Department's legal and practical experiences in enforcing the ADA since 1991. Concurrently with the publication of this final rule for title II, the Department is publishing a final rule amending its ADA title III regulation, which covers nondiscrimination on the basis of disability by public accommodations and in commercial facilities.*

SUPPLEMENTARY INFORMATION:

Enactment of the ADA and Issuance of the 1991 Regulations

*On July 26, 1990, President George H.W. Bush signed into law the ADA, a comprehensive civil rights law prohibiting discrimination on the basis of disability. [1] The ADA broadly protects the rights of individuals with disabilities in employment, access to State and local government services, places of public accommodation, transportation, and other important areas of American life. The ADA also requires newly designed and constructed or altered State and local government facilities, public accommodations, and commercial facilities to be readily accessible to and usable by individuals with disabilities. 42 U.S.C. 12101 et seq. Section 204(a) of the ADA directs the Attorney*

161

General to issue regulations implementing part A of title II but exempts matters within the scope of the authority of the Secretary of Transportation under section 223, 229, or 244. See 42 U.S.C. 12134. Section 229(a) and section 244 of the ADA direct the Secretary of Transportation to issue regulations implementing part B of title II, except for section 223. See 42 U.S.C 12149; 42 U.S.C. 12164. Title II, which this rule addresses, applies to State and local government entities, and, in subtitle A, protects qualified individuals with disabilities from discrimination on the basis of disability in services, programs, and activities provided by State and local government entities. Title II extends the prohibition on discrimination established by section 504 of the Rehabilitation Act of 1973, as amended, 29 U.S.C. 794, to all activities of State and local governments regardless of whether these entities receive Federal financial assistance. 42 U.S.C. 12131B65. ...


On July 26, 1991, the Department issued rules implementing title II and title III, which are codified at 28 CFR part 35 (title II) and part 36 (title III). Appendix A of the 1991 title III regulation, which is republished as Appendix D to 28 CFR part 36, contains the ADA Standards for Accessible Design (1991 Standards), which were based upon the version of theAmericans with Disabilities Act Accessibility Guidelines (1991

*ADAAG) published by the Access Board on the same date. Under the Department's 1991 title III regulation, places of public accommodation and commercial facilities currently are required to comply with the 1991 Standards with respect to newly constructed or altered facilities. The Department's 1991 title II regulation gives public entities the option of complying with the Uniform Federal Accessibility Standards (UFAS) or the 1991 Standards with respect to newly constructed or altered facilities....*

## Relationship to Other Laws

The Department of Justice regulation implementing title II, 28 CFR 35.103, provides the following:

*(b) Other laws.* **This part does not invalidate or limit the remedies, rights, and procedures of any other Federal, State, or local laws (including State common law) that provide greater or equal protection for the rights of individuals with disabilities or individuals associated with them.**

*These provisions remain unchanged by the final rule. The Department recognizes that public entities subject to title II of the ADA may also be subject to title I of the ADA, which prohibits discrimination on the basis of disability in employment; section 504 of the Rehabilitation Act of 1973 and other Federal statutes that prohibit discrimination on the basis of disability in* the programs and activities of recipients of Federal financial assistance; and other Federal statutes such as the Air Carrier Access Act (ACAA), 49 U.S.C. 41705 et seq., and the Fair Housing Act (FHAct), 42 U.S.C. 3601 et seq. Compliance with the Department's title II and title III regulations does not necessarily ensure compliance with other Federal statutes.

Public entities that are subject to the ADA as well as other Federal disability discrimination laws must be aware of the requirements of all applicable laws and must comply with these laws and their implementing regulations. Although in many cases similar provisions of different statutes are interpreted to impose similar requirements, there are circumstances in which similar provisions are applied differently because of the nature of the covered entity or activity or because of distinctions between the statutes. For example, emotional support animals that do not qualify as service animals under the Department's title II regulation may nevertheless qualify as permitted reasonable accommodations for persons with disabilities under the FHAct and the ACAA. See, e.g., Overlook Mutual Homes, Inc. v. Spencer, 666 F. Supp. 2d 850 (S.D. Ohio 2009). Public entities that operate housing facilities must ensure that they apply the reasonable accommodation requirements of the FHAct in determining whether to allow a particular animal *needed by a person with a disability into housing and may not use the ADA definition as a justification for reducing their FHAct obligations. In addition, nothing in the ADA prevents a covered entity subject to one statute from modifying its policies and providing greater access in order to assist individuals with disabilities in achieving access to entities subject to other Federal statutes. For example, a public airport is a title II facility that houses air carriers subject to the ACAA. The public airport operator is required to comply with the title II requirements, but is not covered by the ACAA. Conversely, the air carrier is required to comply with the ACAA, but is not covered by title II of the ADA. If a particular animal is a service animal for purposes of the ACAA and is thus allowed on an airplane, but is not a service animal for purposes of the ADA, nothing in the ADA prohibits an airport from allowing a ticketed passenger with a disability who is traveling with a service animal that meets the ACAA's definition of a service animal to bring that animal into the facility even though under the ADA's definition of service animal the animal could be lawfully excluded.*

## Executive Order 13132

*Title II of the ADA covers State and local government programs, services, and activities and, therefore, clearly has some federalism implications. State and* local governments have been subject to the ADA since 1991, and the majority have also been required to comply with the requirements of section 504. Hence, the ADA and the title II regulation are not novel for State and local governments. In its adoption of the 2010 Standards, the Department was mindful of its obligation to meet the objectives of the ADA while also minimizing conflicts between State law and Federal interests.

## Plain Language Instructions

The Department makes every effort to promote clarity and transparency in its rulemaking. In any regulation, there is a tension between drafting language that is simple and straightforward and drafting language that gives full effect to issues of legal interpretation. The Department operates a toll-free ADA Information Line (800) 514-0301 (voice); (800) 514-0383 (TTY) that the public is welcome to call at any time to obtain assistance in understanding anything in this rule. If any commenter has suggestions for how the regulation could be written more clearly, please contact Janet L. Blizard, Deputy Chief or Barbara J. Elkin, Attorney Advisor, Disability Rights Section, whose contact information is provided in the introductory section of this rule, entitled, "FOR FURTHER INFORMATION CONTACT."

*By the authority vested in me as Attorney General by law, including 28 U.S.C. 509 and 510, 5 U.S.C. 301, and section 204 of the Americans with Disabilities Act of 1990, 101, 42 U.S.C. 12134, and for the reasons set forth in Appendix A to 28 CFR part 35, chapter I of title 28 of the Code of Federal Regulations shall be amended as follows—*

*PART 35—NONDISCRIMINATION ON THE BASIS OF DISABILITY IN STATE AND LOCAL GOVERNMENT SERVICES*

## Section 35.136 Service animals.

*The 1991 title II regulation states that "[a] public entity shall make reasonable modifications in policies, practices, or procedures when the modifications are necessary to avoid discrimination on the basis of disability, unless the public entity can demonstrate that making the modifications would fundamentally alter the nature of the service, program or activity." 28 CFR 130(b)(7). Unlike the title III regulation, the 1991 title II regulation did not contain a specific provision addressing service animals.*

*In the NPRM, the Department stated the intention of providing the broadest feasible access to individuals with disabilities and their service animals, unless a public entity can demonstrate that making the modifications to policies excluding animals would fundamentally alter the nature of the public entity's* service, program, or activity. The Department proposed creating a new § 35.136 addressing service animals that was intended to retain the scope of the 1991 title III regulation at § 36.302(c), while clarifying the Department's longstanding policies and interpretations, as outlined in published technical assistance, Commonly Asked Questions About Service Animals in Places of Business (1996), available at http://www.ada.gov/qasrvc.ftm and ADA Guide for Small Businesses (1999), available at http://www.ada.gov/smbustxt.htm, and to add that a public entity may exclude a service animal in certain circumstances where the service animal fails to meet certain behavioral standards. The Department received extensive comments in response to proposed § 35.136 from individuals, disability advocacy groups, organizations involved in training service animals, and public entities. Those comments and the Department's response are discussed below.

Exclusion of service animals. In the NPRM, the Department proposed incorporating the title III regulatory language of § 36.302(c) into new § 35.136(a), which states that "[g]enerally, a public entity shall modify its policies, practices, or procedures to permit the use of a service animal by an individual with a disability, unless the public entity can demonstrate that the use of a service animal would fundamentally alter the public entity's service,

168

program, or activity." The final rule retains this language with some modifications.

In addition, in the NPRM, the Department proposed clarifying those circumstances where otherwise eligible service animals may be excluded by public entities from their programs or facilities. The Department proposed in § 35.136(b)(1) of the NPRM that a public entity may ask an individual with a disability to remove a service animal from a title II service, program, or activity if: "[t]he animal is out of control and the animal's handler does not take effective action to control it." 73 FR 34466, 34504 (June 17, 2008).

The Department has long held that a service animal must be under the control of the handler at all times. Commenters overwhelmingly were in favor of this language, but noted that there are occasions when service animals are provoked to disruptive or aggressive behavior by agitators or troublemakers, as in the case of a blind individual whose service dog is taunted or pinched. While all service animals are trained to ignore and overcome these types of incidents, misbehavior in response to provocation is not always unreasonable. In circumstances where a service animal misbehaves or responds reasonably to a provocation or injury, the public entity must give the handler a reasonable opportunity to gain control of the animal. Further, if the individual with a disability asserts that the animal was provoked or injured, or if the

169

*public entity otherwise has reason to suspect that provocation or injury has occurred, the public entity should seek to determine the facts and, if provocation or injury occurred, the public entity should take effective steps to prevent further provocation or injury, which may include asking the provocateur to leave the public entity. This language is unchanged in the final rule.*

*The NPRM also proposed language at § 35.136(b)(2) to permit a public entity to exclude a service animal if the animal is not housebroken (i.e., trained so that, absent illness or accident, the animal controls its waste elimination) or the animal's presence or behavior fundamentally alters the nature of the service the public entity provides (e.g., repeated barking during a live performance). Several commenters were supportive of this NPRM language, but cautioned against overreaction by the public entity in these instances. One commenter noted that animals get sick, too, and that accidents occasionally happen. In these circumstances, simple clean up typically addresses the incident. Commenters noted that the public entity must be careful when it excludes a service animal on the basis of "fundamental alteration," asserting for example that a public entity should not exclude a service animal for barking in an environment where other types of noise, such as loud cheering or a child crying, is tolerated. The Department maintains that the appropriateness of an exclusion can be assessed by reviewing how a public entity addresses comparable situations that do not involve a service animal. The Department has retained in § 35.136(b) of the final rule the exception requiring animals to be housebroken. The Department has not retained the specific NPRM language stating that animals can be excluded if their presence or behavior fundamentally alters the nature of the service provided by the public entity, because the Department believes that this exception is covered by the general reasonable modification requirement contained in § 35.130(b)(7). The NPRM also proposed at § 35.136(b)(3) that a service animal can be excluded where "[t]he animal poses a direct threat to the health or safety of others that cannot be eliminated by reasonable modifications." 73 FR 34466, 34504 (June 17, 2008). Commenters were universally supportive of this provision as it makes express the discretion of a public entity to exclude a service animal that poses a direct threat. Several commenters cautioned against the overuse of this provision and suggested that the Department provide an example of the rule's application. The Department has decided not to include regulatory language specifically stating that a service animal can be excluded if it poses a direct threat. The Department believes that the addition of new § 35.139, which incorporates the language of the title III provisions at § 36.302 relating to the general defense of direct threat, is sufficient to establish the availability of this defense to public entities.*

*Access to a public entity following the proper exclusion of a service animal. The NPRM proposed that in the event a public entity properly excludes a service animal, the public entity must give the individual with a disability the opportunity to access the programs, services, and facilities of the public entity without the service animal. Most commenters welcomed this provision as a common sense approach. These commenters noted that they do not wish to preclude individuals with disabilities from the full and equal enjoyment of the State or local government's programs, services, or facilities, simply because of an isolated problem with a service animal. The Department has elected to retain this provision in § 35.136(a).*

*Other requirements. The NPRM also proposed that the regulation include the following requirements: that the work or tasks performed by the service animal must be directly related to the handler's disability; that a service animal must be individually trained to do work or perform a task, be housebroken, and be under the control of the handler; and that a service animal must have a harness, leash, or other tether. Most commenters addressed at least one of these issues in their responses. Most agreed that these provisions are* important to clarify further the 1991 service animal regulation. The Department has moved the requirement that the work or tasks performed by the service animal must be related directly to the handler's disability to the definition of "service animal" in § 35.104. In addition, the Department has modified the proposed language in § 35.136(d) relating to the handler's control of the animal with a harness, leash, or other tether to state that "[a] service animal shall have a harness, leash, or other tether, unless either the handler is unable because of a disability to use a harness, leash, or other tether, or the use of a harness, leash, or other tether would interfere with the service animal's safe, effective performance of work or tasks, in which case the service animal must be otherwise under the handler's control (e.g., voice control, signals, or other effective means)." The Department has retained the requirement that the service animal must be individually trained (see Appendix A discussion of § 35.104, definition of "service animal"), as well as the requirement that the service animal be housebroken.

Responsibility for supervision and care of a service animal. The NPRM proposed language at § 35.136(e) stating that "[a] public entity is not responsible for caring for or supervising a service animal." 73 FR 34466, 34504 (June 17, 2008). Most commenters did not address this particular provision. The Department recognizes that there are occasions when a person with a disability is confined to bed in a hospital for a period of time. In such an instance, the individual may not be able to walk or feed the service animal. In such cases, if the individual has a family member, friend, or other person willing to take on these responsibilities in the place of the individual with disabilities, the individual's obligation to be responsible for the care and supervision of the service animal would be satisfied. The language of this section is retained, with minor modifications, in § 35.136(e) of the final rule.

Inquiries about service animals. The NPRM proposed language at § 35.136(f) setting forth parameters about how a public entity may determine whether an animal qualifies as a service animal. The proposed section stated that a public entity may ask if the animal is required because of a disability and what task or work the animal has been trained to do but may not require proof of service animal certification or licensing. Such inquiries are limited to eliciting the information necessary to make a decision without requiring disclosure of confidential disability-related information that a State or local government entity does not need. This language is consistent with the policy guidance outlined in two Department publications, Commonly Asked Questions about Service Animals in Places of Business (1996), available at http://www.ada.gov/ qasrvc.htm, and ADA Guide for Small Businesses,

*(1999), available at http://www.ada.gov/ smbustxt.htm.*

*Although some commenters contended that the NPRM service animal provisions leave unaddressed the issue of how a public entity can distinguish between a psychiatric service animal, which is covered under the final rule, and a comfort animal, which is not, other commenters noted that the Department's published guidance has helped public entities to distinguish between service animals and pets on the basis of an individual's response to these questions. Accordingly, the Department has retained the NPRM language incorporating its guidance concerning the permissible questions into the final rule.*

*Some commenters suggested that a title II entity be allowed to require current documentation, no more than one year old, on letterhead from a mental health professional stating the following: (1) That the individual seeking to use the animal has a mental health-related disability; (2) that having the animal accompany the individual is necessary to the individual's mental health or treatment or to assist the person otherwise; and (3) that the person providing the assessment of the individual is a licensed mental health professional and the individual seeking to use the animal is under that individual's professional care. These commenters asserted that this will prevent abuse and ensure that individuals with legitimate needs for*

175

psychiatric service animals may use them. The Department believes that this proposal would treat persons with psychiatric, intellectual, and other mental disabilities less favorably than persons with physical or sensory disabilities. The proposal would also require persons with disabilities to obtain medical documentation and carry it with them any time they seek to engage in ordinary activities of daily life in their communities — something individuals without disabilities have not been required to do. Accordingly, the Department has concluded that a documentation requirement of this kind would be unnecessary, burdensome, and contrary to the spirit, intent, and mandates of the ADA.

Areas of a public entity open to the public, participants in services, programs, or activities, or invitees. The NPRM proposed at § 35.136(g) that an individual with a disability who uses a service animal has the same right of access to areas of a title II entity as members of the public, participants in services, programs, or activities, or invitees. Commenters indicated that allowing individuals with disabilities to go with their service animals into the same areas as members of the public, participants in programs, services, or activities, or invitees is accepted practice by most State and local government entities. The Department has included a slightly modified version of this provision in § 35.136(g) of the final rule.

The Department notes that under the final rule, a healthcare facility must also permit a person with a disability to be accompanied by a service animal in all areas of the facility in which that person would otherwise be allowed. There are some exceptions, however. The Department follows the guidance of the Centers for Disease Control and Prevention (CDC) on the use of service animals in a hospital setting. Zoonotic diseases can be transmitted to humans through bites, scratches, direct contact, arthropod vectors, or aerosols.

Consistent with CDC guidance, it is generally appropriate to exclude a service animal from limited-access areas that employ general infection-control measures, such as operating rooms and burn units. See Centers for Disease Control and Prevention, Guidelines for Environmental Infection Control in Health-Care Facilities: Recommendations of CDC and the Healthcare Infection Control Practices Advisory Committee (June 2003), available at http://www.cdc.gov/hicpac/pdf/guidelines/eic_in_HCF_03.pdf (last visited June 24, 2010). A service animal may accompany its handler to such areas as admissions and discharge offices, the emergency room, inpatient and outpatient rooms, examining and diagnostic rooms, clinics, rehabilitation therapy areas, the cafeteria and vending areas, the pharmacy, restrooms, and all other areas of the facility where healthcare personnel, patients, and visitors are permitted without added precaution.

Prohibition against surcharges for use of a service animal. In the NPRM, the Department proposed to incorporate the previously mentioned policy guidance, which prohibits the assessment of a surcharge for the use of a service animal, into proposed § 35.136(h). Several commenters agreed that this provision makes clear the obligation of a public entity to admit an individual with a service animal without surcharges, and that any additional costs imposed should be factored into the overall cost of administering a program, service, or activity, and passed on as a charge to all participants, rather than an individualized surcharge to the service animal user. Commenters also noted that service animal users cannot be required to comply with other requirements that are not generally applicable to other persons. If a public entity normally charges individuals for the damage they cause, an individual with a disability may be charged for damage caused by his or her service animal. The Department has retained this language, with minor modifications, in the final rule at § 35.136(h).

Training requirement. Certain commenters recommended the adoption of formal training requirements for service animals. The Department has rejected this approach and will not impose any type of formal training requirements or certification process, but will continue to require that service animals be individually trained to do work or perform tasks for the benefit of an individual with a disability. While some groups have urged the Department to modify this position, the Department has determined that such a modification would not serve the full array of individuals with disabilities who use service animals, since individuals with disabilities may be capable of training, and some have trained, their service animal to perform tasks or do work to accommodate their disability. A training and certification requirement would increase the expense of acquiring a service animal and might limit access to service animals for individuals with limited financial resources.

Some commenters proposed specific behavior or training standards for service animals, arguing that without such standards, the public has no way to differentiate between untrained pets and service animals. Many of the suggested behavior or training standards were lengthy and detailed. The Department believes that this rule addresses service animal behavior sufficiently by including provisions that address the obligations of the service animal user and the circumstances under which a service animal may be excluded, such as the requirements that an animal be housebroken and under the control of its handler.

Dated: July 23, 2010.

Eric H. Holder, Jr.,

Attorney General.

[FR Doc. 2010-21821 Filed 9-14-10; 8:45 am]

BILLING CODE 4410-14-P

## FOOTNOTES

1. On September 25, 2008, President George W. Bush signed into law the Americans with Disabilities Amendments Act of 2008 (ADA Amendments Act), Public Law 110-325. The ADA Amendments Act amended the ADA definition of disability to clarify its coverage of persons with disabilities and to provide guidance on the application of the definition. This final rule does not contain regulatory language implementing the ADA Amendments Act. The Department intends to publish a supplemental rule to amend the regulatory definition of "disability" to implement the changes mandated by that law.

3. The term "existing facility" is defined in § 35.104 as amended by this rule.

Back to Context

4. The Supreme Court in Tennessee v. Lane, 541 U.S. 509, 533-534 (2004), held that title II of the ADA constitutes a valid exercise of Congress' enforcement power under the Fourteenth Amendment in cases implicating the fundamental right of access to the courts.

*Office of the Federal Register [US]*
*https://www.federalregister.gov/articles/*
*2010/09/15/2010-21821/nondiscrimination-on-the-*
*basis-of-disability-in-state-and-local-government-*
*services#h-51*

*Document below is not in full. Only sections of greater interest to Service Dog Handlers has been copied.*

## Part 35 Nondiscrimination on the Basis of Disability in State and Local Government Services (as amended by the final rule published on September 15, 2010)

Authority: 5 U.S.C. 301; 28 U.S.C. 509, 510; 42 U.S.C. 12134. Billing Code: 4410-1

Subpart A—General

### § 35.101 Purpose.

*The purpose of this part is to effectuate subtitle A of title II of the Americans with Disabilities Act of 1990 (42 U.S. C. 12131), which prohibits discrimination on the basis of disability by public entities.*

### § 35.102 Application.

*(a) Except as provided in paragraph (b) of this section, this part applies to all services, programs, and activities provided or made available by public entities.*

*(b) To the extent that public transportation services, programs, and activities of public entities are covered by subtitle B of title II of the ADA, they are not subject to the requirements of this part.*

*§ 35.103 Relationship to other laws.*

*(a) Rule of interpretation.* Except as otherwise provided in this part, this part shall not be construed to apply a lesser standard than the standards applied under title V of the Rehabilitation Act of 1973 or the regulations issued by Federal agencies pursuant to that title.

*(b) Other laws.* This part does not invalidate or limit the remedies, rights, and procedures of any other Federal laws, or State or local laws (including State common law) that provide greater or equal protection for the rights of individuals with disabilities or individuals associated with them.

## § 35.103 Relationship to other laws.

*(a) Rule of interpretation.* Except as otherwise provided in this part, this part shall not be construed to apply a lesser standard than the standards applied under title V of the Rehabilitation Act of 1973 or the regulations issued by Federal agencies pursuant to that title.

*(b) Other laws.* This part does not invalidate or limit the remedies, rights, and procedures of any other Federal laws, or State or local laws (including State common law) that provide greater or equal protection for the rights of individuals with disabilities or individuals associated with them.

183

## § 35.104 Definitions

*Disability means, with respect to an individual, a physical or mental impairment that substantially limits one or more of the major life activities of such individual; a record of such an impairment; or being regarded as having such an impairment.*

*(1)*

*(i) The phrase physical or mental impairment means—*

*(A) Any physiological disorder or condition, cosmetic disfigurement, or anatomical loss affecting one or more of the following body systems: neurological, musculoskeletal, special sense organs, respiratory (including speech organs), cardiovascular, reproductive, digestive, genitourinary, hemic and lymphatic, skin, and endocrine;*

*(B) Any mental or psychological disorder such as mental retardation, organic brain syndrome, emotional or mental illness, and specific learning disabilities.*

*(ii) The phrase physical or mental impairment includes, but is not limited to, such contagious and noncontagious diseases and conditions as orthopedic, visual, speech and hearing impairments, cerebral palsy, epilepsy, muscular dystrophy, multiple sclerosis, cancer, heart disease, diabetes, mental retardation, emotional illness, specific learning disabilities, HIV disease (whether symptomatic or asymptomatic), tuberculosis, drug addiction, and alcoholism.*

(iii) The phrase physical or mental impairment does not include homosexuality or bisexuality.

(2) The phrase major life activities means functions such as caring for one's self, performing manual tasks, walking, seeing, hearing, speaking, breathing, learning, and working.

(3) The phrase has a record of such an impairment means has a history of, or has been misclassified as having, a mental or physical impairment that substantially limits one or more major life activities.

(4) The phrase is regarded as having an impairment means—

(i) Has a physical or mental impairment that does not substantially limit major life activities but that is treated by a public entity as constituting such a limitation;

(ii) Has a physical or mental impairment that substantially limits major life activities only as a result of the attitudes of others toward such impairment; or

(iii) Has none of the impairments defined in paragraph (1) of this definition but is treated by a public entity as having such an impairment.

(5) The term disability does not include—

(i) Transvestism, transsexualism, pedophilia, exhibitionism, voyeurism, gender identity disorders not resulting from physical impairments, or other sexual behavior disorders;

*(ii) Compulsive gambling, kleptomania, or pyromania; or*

*(iii) Psychoactive substance use disorders resulting from current illegal use of drugs.*

*Housing at a place of education means housing operated by or on behalf of an elementary, secondary, undergraduate, or postgraduate school, or other place of education, including dormitories, suites, apartments, or other places of residence.*

*Public entity means—*

*(1) Any State or local government;*

*(2) Any department, agency, special purpose district, or other instrumentality of a State or States or local government; and*

*(3) The National Railroad Passenger Corporation, and any commuter authority (as defined in section 103(8) of the Rail Passenger Service Act)*

*Qualified individual with a disability means an individual with a disability who, with or without reasonable modifications to rules, policies, or practices, the removal of architectural, communication, or transportation barriers, or the provision of auxiliary aids and services, meets the essential eligibility requirements for the receipt of services or the participation in programs or activities provided by a public entity.*

*Section 504 means section 504 of the Rehabilitation*

Act of 1973 (Pub. L. 93-112, 87 Stat. 394 (29 U.S.C. 794), as amended.

Service animal means any dog that is individually trained to do work or perform tasks for the benefit of an individual with a disability, including a physical, sensory, psychiatric, intellectual, or other mental disability. Other species of animals, whether wild or domestic, trained or untrained, are not service animals for the purposes of this definition. The work or tasks performed by a service animal must be directly related to the individual's disability. Examples of work or tasks include, but are not limited to, assisting individuals who are blind or have low vision with navigation and other tasks, alerting individuals who are deaf or hard of hearing to the presence of people or sounds, providing non-violent protection or rescue work, pulling a wheelchair, assisting an individual during a seizure, alerting individuals to the presence of allergens, retrieving items such as medicine or the telephone, providing physical support and assistance with balance and stability to individuals with mobility disabilities, and helping persons with psychiatric and neurological disabilities by preventing or interrupting impulsive or destructive behaviors. The crime deterrent effects of an animal's presence and the provision of emotional support, well-being, comfort, or companionship do not constitute work or tasks for the purposes of this definition.

187

## § 35.130 General prohibitions against discrimination

*(h) A public entity may impose legitimate safety requirements necessary for the safe operation of its services, programs, or activities. However, the public entity must ensure that its safety requirements are based on actual risks, not on mere speculation, stereotypes, or generalizations about individuals with disabilities.*

## § 35.136 Service animals

*(a) General. Generally, a public entity shall modify its policies, practices, or procedures to permit the use of a service animal by an individual with a disability.*

*(b) Exceptions. A public entity may ask an individual with a disability to remove a service animal from the premises if—*

*(1) The animal is out of control and the animal's handler does not take effective action to control it; or*

*(2) The animal is not housebroken.*

*(c) If an animal is properly excluded. If a public entity properly excludes a service animal under § 35.136(b), it shall give the individual with a disability the opportunity to participate in the service, program, or activity without having the service animal on the premises.*

*(d) Animal under handler's control. A service animal shall be under the control of its handler. A service*

188

*animal shall have a harness, leash, or other tether, unless either the handler is unable because of a disability to use a harness, leash, or other tether, or the use of a harness, leash, or other tether would interfere with the service animal's safe, effective performance of work or tasks, in which case the service animal must be otherwise under the handler's control (e.g., voice control, signals, or other effective means).*

*(e) Care or supervision. A public entity is not responsible for the care or supervision of a service animal.*

*(f) Inquiries. A public entity shall not ask about the nature or extent of a person's disability, but may make two inquiries to determine whether an animal qualifies as a service animal. A public entity may ask if the animal is required because of a disability and what work or task the animal has been trained to perform. A public entity shall not require documentation, such as proof that the animal has been certified, trained, or licensed as a service animal. Generally, a public entity may not make these inquiries about a service animal when it is readily apparent that an animal is trained to do work or perform tasks for an individual with a disability (e.g., the dog is observed guiding an individual who is blind or has low vision, pulling a person's wheelchair, or providing assistance with stability or balance to an individual with an observable mobility disability).*

189

*(g) Access to areas of a public entity. Individuals with disabilities shall be permitted to be accompanied by their service animals in all areas of a public entity's facilities where members of the public, participants in services, programs or activities, or invitees, as relevant, are allowed to go.*

*(h) Surcharges. A public entity shall not ask or require an individual with a disability to pay a surcharge, even if people accompanied by pets are required to pay fees, or to comply with other requirements generally not applicable to people without pets. If a public entity normally charges individuals for the damage they cause, an individual with a disability may be charged for damage caused by his or her service animal.*

## § 35.139 Direct threat.

*(a) This part does not require a public entity to permit an individual to participate in or benefit from the services, programs, or activities of that public entity when that individual poses a direct threat to the health or safety of others.*

*(b) In determining whether an individual poses a direct threat to the health or safety of others, a public entity must make an individualized assessment, based on reasonable judgment that relies on current medical knowledge or on the best available objective evidence, to ascertain: the nature, duration, and severity of the risk; the probability that the potential injury will*

*actually occur; and whether reasonable modifications of policies, practices, or procedures or the provision of auxiliary aids or services will mitigate the risk.*

## Appendix to § 35.151(c)

*(e) Social service center establishments. Group homes, halfway houses, shelters, or similar social service center establishments that provide either temporary sleeping accommodations or residential dwelling units that are subject to this section shall comply with the provisions of the 2010 Standards applicable to residential facilities, including, but not limited to, the provisions in sections 233 and 809.*

*(f) Housing at a place of education. Housing at a place of education that is subject to this section shall comply with the provisions of the 2010 Standards applicable to transient lodging, including, but not limited to, the requirements for transient lodging guest rooms in sections 224 and 806 subject to the following exceptions. For the purposes of the application of this section, the term "sleeping room" is intended to be used interchangeably with the term "guest room" as it is used in the transient lodging standards.*

## Subpart G—Designated Agencies
## § 35.190 Designated Agencies.

*(b) The Federal agencies listed in paragraph (b)(1)-(8) of this section shall have responsibility for the*

*implementation of subpart F of this part for components of State and local governments that exercise responsibilities, regulate, or administer services, programs, or activities in the following functional areas.*

*(6) Department of Justice: All programs, services, and regulatory activities relating to law enforcement, public safety, and the administration of justice, including courts and correctional institutions; commerce and industry, including general economic development, banking and finance, consumer protection, insurance, and small business; planning, development, and regulation (unless assigned to other designated agencies); state and local government support services (e.g., audit, personnel, comptroller, administrative services); all other government functions not assigned to other designated agencies.*

*To read in full go to ada.gov/regs2010/titleII_2010/ titleII_2010_withbold.htm*

## TITLE III (PUBLIC ACCOMODATIONS)

The Department of Justice's regulation implementing title III of the ADA, which prohibits discrimination on the basis of disability in "places of public accommodation" (businesses and non-profit agencies that serve the public) and "commercial facilities" (other businesses). The regulation includes Appendix A to Part 36 - Standards for Accessible Design establishing minimum standards for ensuring accessibility when designing and constructing a new facility or altering an existing facility.

[Federal Register: September 15, 2010 (Volume 75, Number 178)]
[Rules and Regulations] [Page 56236-56358]
DEPARTMENT OF JUSTICE
28 CFR Part 36 [CRT Docket No. 106; AG Order No. 3181-2010]
RIN 1190-AA44

## Nondiscrimination on the Basis of Disability by Public Accommodations and in Commercial Facilities

AGENCY: Department of Justice, Civil Rights Division.

ACTION: Final rule.

SUMMARY:

*This final rule revises the Department of Justice (Department) regulation that implements title III of the Americans with Disabilities Act [[Page 56237]] (ADA), relating to nondiscrimination on the basis of disability by public accommodations and in commercial facilities. The Department is issuing this final rule in order to adopt enforceable accessibility standards under the Americans with Disabilities Act of 1990 (ADA) that are consistent with the minimum guidelines and requirements issued by the Architectural and Transportation Barriers Compliance Board, and to update or amend certain provisions of the title III regulation so that they comport with the Department's legal and practical experiences in enforcing the ADA since 1991. Concurrently with the publication of the final rule for title III, the Department is publishing a final rule amending its ADA title II regulation, which covers nondiscrimination on the basis of disability in State and local government services.*

Effective Date: March 15, 2011.

## Revised definition of Service Animal

*"Service animal means any dog that is individually trained to do work or perform tasks for the benefit of an individual with a disability, including a physical, sensory, psychiatric, intellectual, or other mental disability. Other species of animals, whether wild or domestic, trained or untrained, are*

not service animals for the purposes of this definition. The work or tasks performed by a service animal must be directly related to the handler's disability. Examples of work or tasks include, but are not limited to, assisting individuals who are blind or have low vision with navigation and other tasks, alerting individuals who are deaf or hard of hearing to the presence of people or sounds, providing non-violent protection or rescue work, pulling a wheelchair, assisting an individual during a seizure, alerting individuals to the presence of allergens, retrieving items such as medicine or the telephone, providing physical support and assistance with balance and stability to individuals with mobility disabilities, and helping persons with psychiatric and neurological disabilities by preventing or interrupting impulsive or destructive behaviors. The crime deterrent effects of an animal's presence and the provision of emotional support, well-being, comfort, or companionship do not constitute work or tasks for the purposes of this definition."

Sec. 36.302 Modifications in policies, practices, or procedures.

(c) * * *

*Exceptions. A public accommodation may ask an individual with a disability to remove a service animal from the premises if:*

*(i) The animal is out of control and the animal's handler does not take effective action to control it; or*

*(ii) The animal is not housebroken.*

*If an animal is properly excluded. If a public accommodation properly excludes a service animal under Sec. 36.302(c)(2), it shall give the individual with a disability the opportunity to obtain goods, services, and accommodations without having the service animal on the premises.*

*Animal under handler's control. A service animal shall be under the control of its handler. A service animal shall have a harness, leash, or other tether, unless either the handler is unable because of a disability to use a harness, leash, or other tether, or the use of a harness, leash, or other tether would interfere with the service animal's safe, effective performance of work or tasks, in which case the service animal must be otherwise under the handler's control (e.g., voice control, signals, or other effective means).*

196

*Care or supervision. A public accommodation is not responsible for the care or supervision of a service animal.*

*Inquiries. A public accommodation shall not ask about the nature or extent of a person's disability, but may make two inquiries to determine whether an animal qualifies as a service animal.* **A public accommodation may ask if the animal is required because of a disability and what work or task the animal has been trained to perform. A public accommodation shall not require documentation, such as proof that the animal has been certified, trained, or licensed as a service animal.** *Generally, a public accommodation may not make these inquiries about a service animal when it is readily apparent that an animal is trained to do work or perform tasks for an individual with a disability (e.g., the dog is observed guiding an individual who is blind or has low vision, pulling a person's wheelchair, or providing assistance with stability or balance to an individual with an observable mobility disability).*

*Access to areas of a public accommodation. Individuals with disabilities shall be permitted*

197

to be accompanied by their service animals in all areas of a place of public accommodation where members of the public, program participants, clients, customers, patrons, or invitees, as relevant, are allowed to go.

Surcharges. A public accommodation shall not ask or require an individual with a disability to pay a surcharge, even if people accompanied by pets are required to pay fees, or to comply with other requirements generally not applicable to people without pets. If a public accommodation normally charges individuals for the damage they cause, an individual with a disability may be charged for damage caused by his or her service animal.

Miniature horses. (i) A public accommodation shall make reasonable modifications in policies, practices, or procedures to permit the use of a miniature horse by an individual with a disability if the miniature horse has been individually trained to do work or perform tasks for the benefit of the individual with a disability.

(ii) Assessment factors. In determining whether reasonable modifications in policies, practices, or procedures can be made to allow a miniature horse into a specific facility, a public accommodation shall consider--

The type, size, and weight of the miniature horse and whether the facility can accommodate these features;

Whether the handler has sufficient control of the miniature horse;

Whether the miniature horse is housebroken; and

Whether the miniature horse's presence in a specific facility compromises legitimate safety requirements that are necessary for safe operation.

(iii) Other requirements. Sections 36.302(c)(3) through (c)(8), which apply to service animals, shall also apply to miniature horses.

## Inquiries, Exclusions, Charges, and Other Specific Rules Related to Service Animals

www.ada.gov/service_animals_2010.htm

> When it is not obvious what service an animal provides, only limited inquiries are allowed. Staff may ask two questions: (1) is the dog a service animal required because of a disability, and (2) what work or task has the dog been trained to perform. Staff cannot ask about the person's disability, require medical documentation, require a special identification card or training documentation for the dog, or ask that the dog demonstrate its ability to perform the work or task.

> Allergies and fear of dogs are not valid reasons for denying access or refusing service to people using service animals. When a person who is allergic to dog dander and a person who uses a service animal must spend time in the same room or facility, for example, in a school classroom or at a homeless shelter, they both should be accommodated by assigning them, if possible, to different locations within the room or different rooms in the facility.

A person with a disability cannot be asked to remove his service animal from the premises unless: (1) the dog is out of control and the handler does not take effective action to control it or (2) the dog is not housebroken. When there is a legitimate reason to ask that a service animal be removed, staff must offer the person with the disability the opportunity to obtain goods or services without the animal's presence.

Establishments that sell or prepare food must allow service animals in public areas even if state or local health codes prohibit animals on the premises.

People with disabilities who use service animals cannot be isolated from other patrons, treated less favorably than other patrons, or charged fees that are not charged to other patrons without animals. In addition, if a business requires a deposit or fee to be paid by patrons with pets, it must waive the charge for service animals.

If a business such as a hotel normally charges guests for damage that they cause, a customer with a disability may also be charged for damage caused by himself or his service animal.

*Staff are not required to provide care or food for a service animal.*

## Minimal Protection Change to Non-Violent Protection

NPRM Discussion. Guidance to Revisions of ADA, Definition Change.

> *Providing minimal protection. As previously noted, the 1991 title II regulation does not contain specific language concerning service animals. The 1991 title III regulation included language stating that "minimal protection" was a task that could be performed by an individually trained service animal for the benefit of an individual with a disability. In the Department's "ADA Business Brief on Service Animals" (2002), the Department interpreted the "minimal protection" language within the context of a seizure (i.e., alerting and protecting a person who is having a seizure). The Department received many comments in response to the question of whether the "minimal protection" language should be clarified. Many commenters urged the removal of the "minimal protection" language from the service animal definition for two reasons: (1) The phrase can be interpreted to allow any dog that is trained to be aggressive to qualify as a service animal simply by pairing the animal with a person with a disability; and (2) the phrase can be interpreted to allow any untrained pet dog to qualify as a service animal,*

203

since many consider the mere presence of a dog to be a crime deterrent, and thus sufficient to meet the minimal protection standard. These commenters argued, and the Department agrees, that these interpretations were not contemplated under the original title III regulation, and, for the purposes of the final title II regulations, the meaning of "minimal protection" must be made clear.

While many commenters stated that they believe that the "minimal protection" language should be eliminated, other commenters recommended that the language be clarified, but retained. Commenters favoring clarification of the term suggested that the Department explicitly exclude the function of attack or exclude those animals that are trained solely to be aggressive or protective. Other commenters identified non-violent behavioral tasks that could be construed as minimally protective, such as interrupting self-mutilation, providing safety checks and room searches, reminding the individual to take medications, and protecting the individual from injury resulting from seizures or unconsciousness.

Several commenters noted that the existing direct threat defense, which allows the exclusion of a service animal if the animal exhibits unwarranted or unprovoked violent behavior or poses a direct threat, prevents the use of "attack dogs" as service animals. One commenter noted that the use of a service animal trained to provide "minimal protection" may impede access to care in an emergency, for example, where the first responder, usually a title II entity, is unable or reluctant to approach a person with a disability because the individual's service animal is in a protective posture suggestive of aggression.

Many organizations and individuals stated that in the general dog training community, "protection" is code for attack or aggression training and should be removed from the definition. Commenters stated that there appears to be a broadly held misconception that aggression-trained animals are appropriate service animals for persons with post traumatic stress disorder (PTSD). While many individuals with PTSD may benefit by using a service animal, the work or tasks performed appropriately by such an animal would not involve unprovoked aggression but could include actively cuing the individual by nudging or pawing the individual to alert to the onset of an episode and removing the individual from the anxiety-provoking environment.

*The Department recognizes that despite its best efforts to provide clarification, the "minimal protection" language appears to have been misinterpreted. While the Department maintains that protection from danger is one of the key functions that service animals perform for the benefit of persons with disabilities, the Department recognizes that an animal individually trained to provide aggressive protection, such as an attack dog, is not appropriately considered a service animal. Therefore, the Department has decided to modify the "minimal protection" language to read "non-violent protection," thereby excluding so-called "attack dogs" or dogs with traditional "protection training" as service animals. The Department believes that this modification to the service animal definition will eliminate confusion, without restricting unnecessarily the type of work or tasks that service animals may perform. The Department's modification also clarifies that the crime-deterrent effect of a dog's presence, by itself, does not qualify as work or tasks for purposes of the service animal definition.*

## OTHER FEDERAL AGENCIES WITH ADA RESPONSIBILITIES

Public Transportation - DOT
www.fta.dot.gov/ada

Proposed Design Guidelines- (Access Board)
www.access-board.gov/

Education- (ED)
www.ed.gov/about/offices/list/ocr/index.html

Health Care - (HHS)
www.hhs.gov/ocr/index.html

Labor - (DOL)
www.dol.gov/oasam/programs/crc

Housing - (HUD)
www.hud.gov/offices/fheo/FHLaws/index.cfm

Parks and Recreation - (DOI)
www.doi.gov/diversity/civil_rights.html

Agriculture - (USDA)
www.usda.gov/cr/


In the U.S., the use of service animals may be governed by both federal and state laws. Whichever law grants the greater rights to the individual with a disability will apply when the individual is qualified under both laws. ... Many cases that appear before judges are tried under both federal and state law at the same time.

~ Service Dog Central

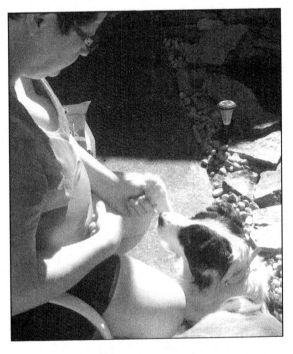

Zoe performing a low blood glucose alert

## HELPFUL CONTACT INFO

TSA Cares (Transportation Security Administration) - For airline travel

TSA Cares toll free number is (855) 787-2227

Active from 9 a.m. to 9 p.m. ET Monday through Friday.

" ... designed to assist travelers in need before they get to the airport. The idea is to answer questions about screening procedures and what the travelers should expect. ... The agency recommends passengers call 72 hours ahead of travel ... "


ADA Questions on Title II and Title III/Dept. of Justice information line at: 800-514-0301 (voice) or 800-514-0383 (TTY)

From the U.S. Department of Justice Civil Rights Division's Disability Rights Section

Quote:

If you feel you or another person have been discriminated against by an entity covered by title III, one of your options is to file a complaint with the federal government. You can send a letter to the U.S. Department of Justice, at the address below, including the following information:

Your full name, address, and telephone number, and the name of the party discriminated against;

The name of the business, organization, or institution that you believe has discriminated;

A description of the act or acts of discrimination, the date or dates of the discriminatory acts, and the name or names of the individuals who you believe discriminated; and

Other information that you believe necessary to support your complaint. Please send copies of relevant documents. Do not send original documents. (Retain them.)

Sign and send the letter to the address below:
U.S. Department of Justice
950 Pennsylvania Avenue, NW
Civil Rights Division
Disability Rights - NYAVE
Washington, D.C. 20530

From the ADA Website:
You may also file a complaint by E-mail at ADA.complaint@usdoj.gov.

If you have questions about filing an ADA complaint, please call: ADA Information Line: 800-514-0301 (voice) or 800-514-0383 (TTY).

Main Section Telephone Number: 202-307-0663 (voice and TTY)

Arrow at Epcot, Disney World

## EMPLOYMENT

The agency overseeing employment issues is the EEOC, the U.S. Equal Employment Opportunity Commission.

### The U.S. Equal Employment Opportunity Commission

eeoc.gov

*Title I of the Americans with Disabilities Act of 1990 (ADA) makes it unlawful for an employer to discriminate against a qualified applicant or employee with a disability. The ADA applies to private employers with 15 or more employees and to state and local government employers. The U.S. Equal Employment Opportunity Commission (EEOC) enforces the employment provisions of the ADA.*

*The ADA prohibits employers from asking questions that are likely to reveal the existence of a disability before making a job offer (i.e., the pre-offer period). This prohibition covers written questionnaires and inquiries made during interviews, as well as medical examinations. However, such questions and medical examinations are permitted after extending a job offer but before the individual begins work (i.e., the post-offer period).*

*An applicant with a disability, like all other applicants, must be able to meet the employer's requirements for the job, such as education, training, employment experience, skills, or licenses. In addition, an applicant with a disability must be able to perform the "essential functions" of the job the fundamental duties either on her own or with the help of "reasonable accommodation." However, an employer does not have to provide a reasonable accommodation that will cause "undue hardship," which is significant difficulty or expense.*

## Disability Discrimination

*Disability discrimination occurs when an employer or other entity covered by the Americans with Disabilities Act, as amended, or the Rehabilitation Act, as amended, treats a qualified individual with a disability who is an employee or applicant unfavorably because she has a disability.*

*Disability discrimination also occurs when a covered employer or other entity treats an applicant or employee less favorably because she has a history of a disability (such as cancer that is controlled or in remission) or because she is believed to have a physical or mental impairment that is not transitory (lasting or expected to last six months or less) and minor (even if she does not have such an impairment).*

213

*The law requires an employer to provide reasonable accommodation to an employee or job applicant with a disability, unless doing so would cause significant difficulty or expense for the employer ("undue hardship").*

*The law also protects people from discrimination based on their relationship with a person with a disability (even if they do not themselves have a disability). For example, it is illegal to discriminate against an employee because her husband has a disability.*

*Note: Federal employees and applicants are covered by the Rehabilitation Act of 1973, instead of the Americans with Disabilities Act. The protections are mostly the same.*

## Definition Of Disability

*Not everyone with a medical condition is protected by the law. In order to be protected, a person must be qualified for the job and have a disability as defined by the law.*

*A person can show that he or she has a disability in one of three ways:*

*A person may be disabled if he or she has a physical or mental condition that substantially*

214

*limits a major life activity (such as walking, talking, seeing, hearing, or learning).*

*A person may be disabled if he or she has a history of a disability (such as cancer that is in remission).*

*A person may be disabled if he is believed to have a physical or mental impairment that is not transitory (lasting or expected to last six months or less) and minor (even if he does not have such an impairment).*

## To obtain more information about the ADA, contact the EEOC at:

1-800-669-4000 (voice)
1-800-669-6820 (TTY)

*All calls are confidential*

## JOB ACCOMMODATION NETWORK (JAN)

The Job Accommodation Network (JAN) is the leading source of free, expert, and confidential guidance on workplace accommodations and disability employment issues.

askjan.org

Connect with JAN:

(800)526-7234 (voice)

(877)781-9403 (TTY)

**Effective Accommodation Practices**
**JAN'S (EAP) SERIES**
DOS AND DON'TS OF DISCLOSURE

Quote:

*Disclosing a disability may be a consideration when starting a new job; transitioning from school, another job, or unemployment; or retaining a job after acquiring a disability. For individuals who may still be struggling with accepting their medical condition, making the decision to disclose can be overwhelming. Because some impairments are not visible, individuals may face such challenges as understanding their impairments and determining what types of accommodations are available. As with any new experience, preparation is vital. The following provides* an overview of the do's and don'ts of disclosure. Note that disclosing is a very personal decision, but some of the following tips may be helpful in making that decision. Contact JAN for additional information related to job accommodations, the Americans with Disabilities Act (ADA), and other resources.

## INTERNAL REVENUE SERVICE (IRS)
## IRS Service Dog Deductions

*Guide Dog or Other Service Animal*

*You can include in medical expenses the costs of buying, training, and maintaining a guide dog or other service animal to assist a visually impaired or hearing disabled person, or a person with other physical disabilities. In general, this includes any costs, such as food, grooming, and veterinary care, incurred in maintaining the health and vitality of the service animal so that it may perform its duties.*

Department of the Treasury
Internal Revenue Service
Publication 502
Medical and Dental Expenses

# FLORIDA STATE INFORMATION

Information of FL State Statutes has been inserted with this additional section. Readers from other states can benefit from the extra knowledge and information given and used in this area as a lesson in reading state statutes.

Zoe

Florida Attorney General
State of Florida
The Capitol PL-01
Tallahassee, FL 32399-1050
Citizens Services: 850-414-3990
Florida Relay/TDD: 800-955-8771
Florida Toll Free: 1-866-966-7226
ag.mccollum@myfloridalegal.com

Florida Commission on Human Relations
325 John Knox Road, Bldg. F, Suite 240
Tallahassee, FL 32303-4149
IN FL (800) 342-8170
Tel: (904) 488-7082
Fax: (904) 488-5291
TTY: (800) 955-8770

Zoe

# FLORIDA STATE STATUTES

## During Disasters and Emergencies

### 252.355 f.s. – Registry of persons with special needs

(1) In order to meet the special needs of persons who would need assistance during evacuations and sheltering because of physical, mental, cognitive impairment, or sensory disabilities, each local emergency management agency in the state shall maintain a registry of persons with special needs located within the jurisdiction of the local agency. The registration shall identify those persons in need of assistance and plan for resource allocation to meet those identified needs. To assist the local emergency management agency in identifying such persons, home health agencies, hospices, nurse registries, home medical equipment providers, the Department of Children and Family Services, Department of Health, Agency for Health Care Administration, Department of Education, Agency for Persons with Disabilities, and Department of Elderly Affairs shall provide registration information to all of their special needs clients and to all persons with special needs who receive services. The registry shall be updated annually. The

*registration program shall give persons with special needs the option of preauthorizing emergency response personnel to enter their homes during search and rescue operations if necessary to assure their safety and welfare following disasters.*

*(2) The division shall be the designated lead agency responsible for community education and outreach to the public, including special needs clients, regarding registration and special needs shelters and general information regarding shelter stays.*

*(3) A person with special needs must be allowed to bring his or her service animal into a special needs shelter in accordance with s. 413.08.*

*Special Attention Note: According to FL Statutes a person with special needs must be allowed to bring their service animal (dog) into what is officially known as "A Special Needs Shelter". This does not mean that any person with a legal disability must go to such a shelter as they are not automatically considered having special needs. Person with Legal Disability does not equal person with special needs. Most people with a disability and using an Assistance/Service Dog will go to a regular "Mass Care Shelter" such as opened and run by the American Red Cross. The Public Access Right of someone with a legal disability allows such a* person to go into community emergency shelters with a dog trained to mitigate their disability per the Department of Justice.

**316.1303f.s. Traffic regulations to assist mobility-impaired persons.** — Whenever a pedestrian is in the process of crossing a public street or highway and the pedestrian is mobility-impaired (using a guide dog or service animal designated as such with a visible means of identification, a walker, a crutch, an orthopedic cane, or a wheelchair), the driver of every vehicle approaching the intersection, as defined in s. 316.003(17), shall bring his or her vehicle to a full stop before ...

**413.08 Rights and responsibilities of an individual with a disability; use of a service animal; prohibited discrimination in public employment, public accommodations, and housing accommodations; penalties.** —

(1) As used in this section and s. 413.081, the term:

(a) "Housing accommodation" means any real property or portion thereof which is used or occupied, or intended, arranged, or designed to be used or occupied, as the home, residence, or sleeping place of one or more persons, but does not include any single-family residence, the occupants of which rent, lease, or furnish for compensation not more than one room therein.

(b)  "Individual with a disability" means a person who has a physical or mental impairment that substantially limits one or more major life activities of the individual. As used in this paragraph, the term:

1.  "Major life activity" means a function such as caring for one's self, performing manual tasks, walking, seeing, hearing, speaking, breathing, learning, and working.

2.  "Physical or mental impairment" means:

a.  A physiological disorder or condition, disfigurement, or anatomical loss that affects one or more bodily functions; or

b.  A mental or psychological disorder that meets one of the diagnostic categories specified in the most recent edition of the Diagnostic and Statistical Manual of Mental Disorders published by the American Psychiatric Association, such as an intellectual or developmental disability, organic brain syndrome, traumatic brain injury, posttraumatic stress disorder, or an emotional or mental illness.

(c) "Public accommodation" means a common carrier, airplane, motor vehicle, railroad train, motor bus, streetcar, boat, or other public conveyance or mode of transportation; hotel; a timeshare that is a transient public lodging establishment as defined in s. 509.013; lodging place; place of public accommodation, amusement, or resort; and other places to which the general public is invited, subject only to the conditions and limitations established by law and applicable alike to all persons. The term does not include air carriers covered by the Air Carrier Access Act of 1986, 49 U.S.C. s. 41705, and by regulations adopted by the United States Department of Transportation to implement such act.

(d) "Service animal" means an animal that is trained to do work or perform tasks for an individual with a disability, including a physical, sensory, psychiatric, intellectual, or other mental disability. The work done or tasks performed must be directly related to the individual's disability and may include, but are not limited to, guiding an individual who is visually impaired or blind, alerting an individual who is deaf or hard of

225

hearing, pulling a wheelchair, assisting with mobility or balance, alerting and protecting an individual who is having a seizure, retrieving objects, alerting an individual to the presence of allergens, providing physical support and assistance with balance and stability to an individual with a mobility disability, helping an individual with a psychiatric or neurological disability by preventing or interrupting impulsive or destructive behaviors, reminding an individual with mental illness to take prescribed medications, calming an individual with posttraumatic stress disorder during an anxiety attack, or doing other specific work or performing other special tasks. A service animal is not a pet. For purposes of subsections (2), (3), and (4), the term "service animal" is limited to a dog or miniature horse. The crime-deterrent effect of an animal's presence and the provision of emotional support, well-being, comfort, or companionship do not constitute work or tasks for purposes of this definition.

(2) An individual with a disability is entitled to full and equal accommodations, advantages, facilities, and privileges in all public accommodations. A public accommodation must modify its policies, practices, and procedures to permit use of a service animal by an individual

226

with a disability. This section does not require any person, firm, business, or corporation, or any agent thereof, to modify or provide any vehicle, premises, facility, or service to a higher degree of accommodation than is required for a person not so disabled.

(3)    An individual with a disability has the right to be accompanied by a service animal in all areas of a public accommodation that the public or customers are normally permitted to occupy.

(a)    The service animal must be under the control of its handler and must have a harness, leash, or other tether, unless either the handler is unable because of a disability to use a harness, leash, or other tether, or the use of a harness, leash, or other tether would interfere with the service animal's safe, effective performance of work or tasks, in which case the service animal must be otherwise under the handler's control by means of voice control, signals, or other effective means.

(b)    Documentation that the service animal is trained is not a precondition for providing service to an individual accompanied by a service animal. A public accommodation may not ask about the nature or extent of an individual's disability. To determine the difference between a service animal and a pet, a public accommodation may ask if an animal is a service animal required because of a disability and what work or tasks the animal has been trained to perform.

(c)   A public accommodation may not impose a deposit or surcharge on an individual with a disability as a precondition to permitting a service animal to accompany the individual with a disability, even if a deposit is routinely required for pets.

(d)   An individual with a disability is liable for damage caused by a service animal if it is the regular policy and practice of the public accommodation to charge nondisabled persons for damages caused by their pets.

(e)   The care or supervision of a service animal is the responsibility of the individual owner. A public accommodation is not required to provide care or food or a special location for the service animal or assistance with removing animal excrement.

(f)   A public accommodation may exclude or remove any animal from the premises, including a service animal, if the animal is out of control and the animal's handler does not take effective action to control it, the animal is not housebroken, or the animal's behavior poses a direct threat to the health and safety of others. Allergies and fear of animals are not valid reasons for denying access or refusing service to an individual with a service animal. If a service animal is excluded or removed for being a direct threat to others, the public accommodation must provide the individual with a disability the option of continuing access to the public accommodation without having the service animal on the premises.

(4) Any person, firm, or corporation, or the agent of any person, firm, or corporation, who denies or interferes with admittance to, or enjoyment of, a public accommodation or, with regard to a public accommodation, otherwise interferes with the rights of an individual with a disability or the trainer of a service animal while engaged in the training of such an animal pursuant to subsection (8), commits a misdemeanor of the second degree, punishable as provided in s. 775.082 or s. 775.083 and must perform 30 hours of community service for an organization that serves individuals with disabilities, or for another entity or organization at the discretion of the court, to be completed in not more than 6 months.

(5) It is the policy of this state that an individual with a disability be employed in the service of the state or political subdivisions of the state, in the public schools, and in all other employment

*supported in whole or in part by public funds, and an employer may not refuse employment to such a person on the basis of the disability alone, unless it is shown that the particular disability prevents the satisfactory performance of the work involved.*

*(6) An individual with a disability is entitled to rent, lease, or purchase, as other members of the general public, any housing accommodations offered for rent, lease, or other compensation in this state, subject to the conditions and limitations established by law and applicable alike to all persons.*

*(a) This section does not require any person renting, leasing, or otherwise providing real property for compensation to modify her or his property in any way or provide a higher degree of care for an individual with a disability than for a person who is not disabled.*

*(b) An individual with a disability who has a service animal or who obtains a service animal is entitled to full and equal access to all housing accommodations provided for in this section, and such a person may not be required to pay extra compensation for such animal. However, such a person is liable for any damage done to the premises or to another person on the premises by the animal. A housing accommodation may*

request proof of compliance with vaccination requirements.

(c) This subsection does not limit the rights or remedies of a housing accommodation or an individual with a disability that are granted by federal law or another law of this state with regard to other assistance animals.

(7) An employer covered under subsection (5) who discriminates against an individual with a disability in employment, unless it is shown that the particular disability prevents the satisfactory performance of the work involved, or any person, firm, or corporation, or the agent of any person, firm, or corporation, providing housing accommodations as provided in subsection (6) who discriminates against an individual with a disability, commits a misdemeanor of the second degree, punishable as provided in s. 775.082 or s. 775.083.

(8) Any trainer of a service animal, while engaged in the training of such an animal, has the same rights and privileges with respect to access to public facilities and the same liability for damage as is provided for those persons described in subsection (3) accompanied by service animals.

231

*(9) A person who knowingly and willfully misrepresents herself or himself, through conduct or verbal or written notice, as using a service animal and being qualified to use a service animal or as a trainer of a service animal commits a misdemeanor of the second degree, punishable as provided in s. 775.082 or s. 775.083 and must perform 30 hours of community service for an organization that serves individuals with disabilities, or for another entity or organization at the discretion of the court, to be completed in not more than 6 months.*

### 509.013f.s.   Lodging and Food.   Definitions. —
### As used in this chapter, the term:

*(1)   "Division" means the Division of Hotels and Restaurants of the Department of Business and Professional Regulation.*

*(2)   "Operator" means the owner, licensee, proprietor, lessee, manager, assistant manager, or*

appointed agent of a public lodging establishment or public food service establishment.

*(3)* *"Guest" means any patron, customer, tenant, lodger, boarder, or occupant of a public lodging establishment or public food service establishment.*

*(4)(a)* *"Public lodging establishment" includes a transient public lodging establishment as defined in subparagraph 1. and a nontransient public lodging establishment as defined in subparagraph 2.*

*1.* *"Transient public lodging establishment" means any unit, group of units, dwelling, building, or group of buildings within a single complex of buildings which is rented to guests more than three times in a calendar year for periods of less than 30 days or 1 calendar month, whichever is less, or which is advertised or held out to the public as a place regularly rented to guests.*

*2.* *"Nontransient public lodging establishment" means any unit, group of units, dwelling, building, or group of buildings within a single complex of buildings which is rented to guests for periods of at least 30 days or 1 calendar month, whichever is less, or which is advertised or held out to the public as a place regularly rented to guests for periods of at least 30 days or 1 calendar month.*

*License classifications of public lodging establishments, and the definitions therefor, are set out in s. 509.242. For the purpose of licensure, the term does not include condominium common elements as defined in s. 718.103.*

*(b) The following are excluded from the definitions in paragraph (a):*

*1. Any dormitory or other living or sleeping facility maintained by a public or private school, college, or university for the use of students, faculty, or visitors.*

*2. Any facility certified or licensed and regulated by the Agency for Health Care Administration or the Department of Children and Families or other similar place regulated under s. 381.0072.*

*3. Any place renting four rental units or less, unless the rental units are advertised or held out to the public to be places that are regularly rented to transients.*

*4. Any unit or group of units in a condominium, cooperative, or timeshare plan and any individually or collectively owned one-family, two-family, three-family, or four-family dwelling house or dwelling unit that is rented for periods of at least 30 days or 1 calendar month, whichever is less,* and that is not advertised or held out to the public as a place regularly rented for periods of less than 1 calendar month, provided that no more than four rental units within a single complex of buildings are available for rent.

5. Any migrant labor camp or residential migrant housing permitted by the Department of Health under ss. 381.008-381.00895.

6. Any establishment inspected by the Department of Health and regulated by chapter 513.

7. Any nonprofit organization that operates a facility providing housing only to patients, patients' families, and patients' caregivers and not to the general public.

8. Any apartment building inspected by the United States Department of Housing and Urban Development or other entity acting on the department's behalf that is designated primarily as housing for persons at least 62 years of age. The division may require the operator of the apartment building to attest in writing that such building meets the criteria provided in this subparagraph. The division may adopt rules to implement this requirement.

9. Any roominghouse, boardinghouse, or other living or sleeping facility that may not be classified as a hotel, motel, timeshare project, vacation rental, nontransient apartment, bed and breakfast inn, or transient apartment under s. 509.242.

(5)(a) "Public food service establishment" means any building, vehicle, place, or structure, or any room or division in a building, vehicle, place, or structure where food is prepared, served, or sold for immediate consumption on or in the vicinity of the premises; called for or taken out by customers; or prepared prior to being delivered to another location for consumption.

(b) The following are excluded from the definition in paragraph (a):

1. Any place maintained and operated by a public or private school, college, or university:

a. For the use of students and faculty; or

b. Temporarily to serve such events as fairs, carnivals, and athletic contests.

2. Any eating place maintained and operated by a church or a religious, nonprofit fraternal, or nonprofit civic organization:

a. For the use of members and associates; or

*b.* Temporarily to serve such events as fairs, carnivals, or athletic contests.

*3.* Any eating place located on an airplane, train, bus, or watercraft which is a common carrier.

*4.* Any eating place maintained by a facility certified or licensed and regulated by the Agency for Health Care Administration or the Department of Children and Families or other similar place that is regulated under s. 381.0072.

*5.* Any place of business issued a permit or inspected by the Department of Agriculture and Consumer Services under s. 500.12.

*6.* Any place of business where the food available for consumption is limited to ice, beverages with or without garnishment, popcorn, or prepackaged items sold without additions or preparation.

*7.* Any theater, if the primary use is as a theater and if patron service is limited to food items customarily served to the admittees of theaters.

*8.* Any vending machine that dispenses any food or beverages other than potentially hazardous foods, as defined by division rule.

9. Any vending machine that dispenses potentially hazardous food and which is located in a facility regulated under s. 381.0072.

10. Any research and development test kitchen limited to the use of employees and which is not open to the general public.

(6) "Director" means the Director of the Division of Hotels and Restaurants of the Department of Business and Professional Regulation.

(7) "Single complex of buildings" means all buildings or structures that are owned, managed, controlled, or operated under one business name and are situated on the same tract or plot of land that is not separated by a public street or highway.

(8) "Temporary food service event" means any event of 30 days or less in duration where food is prepared, served, or sold to the general public.

(9) "Theme park or entertainment complex" means a complex comprised of at least 25 contiguous acres owned and controlled by the same business entity and which contains permanent exhibitions and a variety of recreational activities and has a minimum of 1 million visitors annually.

(10) "Third-party provider" means, for purposes of s. 509.049, any provider of an approved food

safety training program that provides training or such a training program to a public food service establishment that is not under common ownership or control with the provider.

*(11)* "Transient establishment" means any public lodging establishment that is rented or leased to guests by an operator whose intention is that such guests' occupancy will be temporary.

*(12)* "Transient occupancy" means occupancy when it is the intention of the parties that the occupancy will be temporary. There is a rebuttable presumption that, when the dwelling unit occupied is not the sole residence of the guest, the occupancy is transient.

*(13)* "Transient" means a guest in transient occupancy.

*(14)* "Nontransient establishment" means any public lodging establishment that is rented or leased to guests by an operator whose intention is that the dwelling unit occupied will be the sole residence of the guest.

*(15)* "Nontransient occupancy" means occupancy when it is the intention of the parties that the occupancy will not be temporary. There is a rebuttable presumption that, when the dwelling

*unit occupied is the sole residence of the guest, the occupancy is nontransient.*

*(16) "Nontransient" means a guest in nontransient occupancy.*

*History.—s. 1, ch. 73-325; s. 3, ch. 76-168; s. 1, ch. 77-457; ss. 1, 39, 42, ch. 79-240; ss. 3, 4, ch. 81-161; ss. 2, 3, ch. 81-318; s. 2, ch. 83-241; s. 3, ch. 87-117; s. 31, ch. 88-90; s. 2, ch. 88-275; ss. 2, 51, 52, ch. 90-339; s. 1, ch. 91-40; s. 4, ch. 91-429; s. 21, ch. 92-180; s. 1, ch. 93-53; s. 14, ch. 93-133; s. 36, ch. 94-180; s. 202, ch. 94-218; s. 42, ch. 95-210; s. 3, ch. 95-314; s. 2, ch. 96-384; s. 245, ch. 99-8; s. 7, ch. 2004-292; s. 1, ch. 2008-55; s. 25, ch. 2010-161; s. 1, ch. 2011-119; s. 1, ch. 2012-165; s. 275, ch. 2014-19; s. 1, ch. 2014-133.*

## Statute 767.16 Bite by a police or service dog; exemption from quarantine.

*767.16 Bite by a police or service dog; exemption from quarantine.—Any dog that is owned, or the service of which is employed, by a law enforcement agency, or any dog that is used as a service dog for blind, hearing impaired, or disabled persons, and that bites another animal or human is exempt from any quarantine requirement following* such bite if the dog has a current rabies vaccination that was administered by a licensed veterinarian.

775.082f.s. Penalties; applicability of sentencing structures; mandatory minimum sentences for certain reoffenders previously released from prison. —

(4)(b) For a misdemeanor of the second degree, by a definite term of imprisonment not exceeding 60 days.

775.083f.s. Fines.

(1) A person who has been convicted of an offense other than a capital felony may be sentenced to pay a fine in addition to any punishment described in s. 775.082; when specifically authorized by statute, he or she may be sentenced to pay a fine in lieu of any punishment described in s. 775.082. A person who has been convicted of a noncriminal violation may be sentenced to pay a fine. Fines for designated crimes and for noncriminal violations shall not exceed:

...

*(e)  $500, when the conviction is of a misdemeanor of the second degree or a noncriminal violation.*

## SERVICE DOGS IN FLORIDA SCHOOLS

Any student   that wishes to attend school together with their dog needs to learn the proper manner in which to make such a request. Minors will need to have their parent(s) or other legal guardian handle this procedure. This new guidance is now compliant with the Dept. of Justice / ADA Title II.

The following document is not printed in its entirety here. Specific quotes are printed below and those with an interest in this topic are encouraged to read the document in full.

### Nondiscrimination on the Basis of Disability in State and Local Government Services

Florida Department of Education

Bureau of Exceptional Education and Student Services

Updated Guidelines and Template for School District Policy,

Practice and Procedures for the

Use of Service Animals by Students with Disabilities

2015

On March 15, 2011, the U.S. Department of Justice (DOJ) finalized regulations promulgated under Title II of the Americans with Disabilities Act (ADA) regarding the use of service animals in governmental settings, including public schools. Before the ADA regulations became final, the Governor's Commission on Disabilities recommended in 2010 that the Florida Department of Education (FDOE) provide guidance to school districts addressing this issue. As a result, FDOE issued initial guidance to school districts in August 2010. Since that initial guidance was issued, however, further guidance has been provided by courts, the Office for Civil Rights (OCR) and DOJ that impacts the initial guidance provided by FDOE. Therefore, these updated guidelines are necessary, and the initial guidance issued in August 2010 should not be used at this time. (See Note 1)

Legal Sources and References

The information provided in these Guidelines relies on the legal standards as set forth in Title II of the ADA and its regulations. The ADA is a federal civil rights law prohibiting discrimination on the basis of disability. Thus, the primary legal references herein will be the ADA and its Title II regulations, as well as a Guidance and Analysis document issued by the DOJ on September 15, 2010. Also relied upon will be current court, OCR and DOJ interpretations of the ADA's requirements as they relate to the use of service animals by students with disabilities.

In addition, the following introductory and overriding principles should be considered for incorporation into procedures and training.

• There are only two questions that may be asked and answered when a request to allow a student to bring his or her service animal to school is made: 1) whether the student for whom the request is made is an individual with a disability; and 2) whether the service animal meets the definition of "service animal" under the law. A student determined to be a student with a disability under the IDEA or Section 504 would be an individual with a disability.

• According to OCR and DOJ, whether a student with a disability may bring his or her service animal to school does not depend upon whether the animal is necessary to provide the student FAPE (e.g., it does not matter that the student's paraprofessional can provide the student the same assistance).

• The fact that other students or school staff have allergies to, or a fear of the animal, is not relevant to the inquiry, according to DOJ.

• Under the ADA, service animals must be harnessed, leashed or tethered, unless these devices interfere with the service animal's work, or the individual's disability prevents the use of these devices. In that case, the individual must maintain control of the animal through voice, signal or other effective controls.

245

• Certification or proof of service animal training, licensing or things such as immunization beyond the required rabies vaccination (See Note 4) , health or cleanliness cannot be required    in the process of determining whether a request will be granted. However, such information may be requested.

• The only allowable reasons for denying a proper request for a service animal to attend school with a student with a disability or asking that a service animal be removed from school premises are: 1) the animal is out of control and the animal's handler does not take effective action to control it; 2) the animal is not housebroken; 3) the animal's presence poses a "direct threat" to the health or safety of others, based upon an individualized assessment; or 4) the animal's presence would constitute a "fundamental alteration" to the nature of the services, program or activity provided by the school. (See Note 5)

Notes:

1 It is important to note that employees also make requests to bring service animals to school. Accommodating an employee's request, however, is beyond the scope of this guidance.
4 § 828.30, Florida Statutes.

5 §§ 35.130(b)(7), 35.139; 28 C.F.R. pt.35, app. A, § 35.104 at 600, §35.136 at 608 (July 1, 2014).

info.fldoe.org/docushare/dsweb/Get/Document-7346/dps-2015-60a.pdf

For further reading and understanding is a 2015 case that involved a minor child and the School board of Broward County.

MONICA ALBONIGA, individually and on behalf of A.M., a minor, Plaintiff,

v.

THE SCHOOL BOARD OF BROWARD COUNTY FLORIDA, Defendant.

Case No. 14-CIV-60085-BLOOM/Valle.

United States District Court, S.D. Florida.

February 10, 2015.

DREAM DOGZ - SERVICE DOGS

## THERAPY DOG

> *Therapy animals and their handlers are trained to provide specific human populations with appropriate contact with animals. They are usually the personal pets of the handlers and accompany their handlers to the sites they visit, but therapy animals may also reside at a facility. Animals must meet specific criteria for health, grooming and behavior. While managed by their handlers, their work is not handler-focused and instead provides benefits to others.*

~ Delta Society


The owner/handler of a Therapy Dog does not have additional rights in Housing or Public Access over any other pet owner.

Therapy Dogs are not Assistance or Service Dogs. Therapy Dogs are pet dogs with special training and of the proper temperament to work with their owner around and for other people. Therapy Dogs can be owned by either disabled or non-disabled owners.

Most national organizations register their teams but do not certify them. A registered team may or may not have gone through training with a specific organization. The registration of the team in most cases means that the team signed up, paid a testing fee along with submitting an application, and went for an evaluation. If they passed their evaluation (test) with a set minimum score they then were eligible to be registered with that organization.

When a team is *certified* that implies that the organization requires certain training (classes through them) over a recognized length of time, normally has additional requirements like a minimum number of supervised visits, and possibly several different tests. This particular organization then certifies that the team has met their standards. There are fewer organizations that certify as it requires a more in-depth relationship between the team and the organization. Certifying organizations normally also monitor the team to make sure they are complying with their regulations and in some cases also mentor and do additional training with their teams.

Arrow

## EMOTIONAL SUPPORT DOG (ANIMAL)

> *An Emotional Support Animal is a dog or other common domestic animal that provides therapeutic support to a disabled or elderly owner through companionship, non-judgmental positive regard, affection, and a focus in life. If a doctor determines that a patient with a disabling mental illness would benefit from the companionship of an emotional support animal, the doctor write letters supporting a request by the patient to keep the ESA in "no pets" housing or to travel with the ESA in the cabin of an aircraft.*

~ Service Dog Central

If your treating doctor or medical team decide that you have a disabling mental illness and enters such into your medical records then you may be able to have your dog live with you in no-pet housing. Only landlords in certain types of housing are required to accommodate you and allow your dog to live in the rental.

## POSITION ON BREED BANS

*The Dept. of Justice has in their appendix to 28 CFR Part 36 given their opinion on breed bans. Note: This opinion while it may carry weight in a court trial is not part of DOJ regulatory law. In the future this opinion and rulings by the courts may lead to protection under Case Law. People deciding on using any dog listed on a breed ban at this time still do so at their own risk if living or traveling in areas with breed bans.*

*Breed limitations. A few commenters suggested that certain breeds of dogs should not be allowed to be used as service animals. Some suggested that the Department should defer to local laws restricting the breeds of dogs that individuals who reside in a community may own. Other commenters opposed breed restrictions, stating that the breed of a dog does not determine its propensity for aggression and that aggressive and non-aggressive dogs exist in all breeds.*

*The Department does not believe that it is either appropriate or consistent with the ADA to defer to local laws that prohibit certain breeds of dogs based on local concerns that these breeds may*

251

*have a history of unprovoked aggression or attacks. Such deference would have the effect of limiting the rights of persons with disabilities under the ADA who use certain service animals based on where they live rather than on whether the use of a particular animal poses a direct threat to the health and safety of others. Breed restrictions differ significantly from jurisdiction to jurisdiction. Some jurisdictions have no breed restrictions. Others have restrictions that, while well-meaning, have the unintended effect of screening out the very breeds of dogs that have successfully served as service animals for decades without a history of the type of unprovoked aggression or attacks that would pose a direct threat, e.g., German Shepherds. Other jurisdictions prohibit animals over a certain weight, thereby restricting breeds without invoking an express breed ban. In addition, deference to breed restrictions contained in local laws would have the unacceptable consequence of restricting travel by an individual with a disability who uses a breed that is acceptable and poses no safety hazards in the individual's home jurisdiction but is nonetheless banned by other jurisdictions. Public accommodations have the ability to determine, on a case-by- case basis, whether a particular service animal can be excluded based on that particular animal's actual behavior or history--not based on* fears or generalizations about how an animal or breed might behave. This ability to exclude an animal whose behavior or history evidences a direct threat is sufficient to protect health and safety.

## Theresa A. Jennings

Founder and Executive Director Of Karl's Kids Program, Inc.

The mission of Karl's Kids Program, Inc. is to educate on safety topics; to assist children, teens, young adults, and people with disabilities in having a good quality of life; and to promote family and community values through various means including but not limited to the natural bond between a person and an animal, primarily that of the dog.

Assistance Dog Advocacy Project (ADAP) is a project of Karl's Kids Program, Inc. The majority of volunteers with ADAP are themselves Assistance Dog handlers and/or trainers.

Besides working with Karl's Kids Program, Inc., Theresa is involved in various other volunteer and non-profit activities.

Founder and Executive Director of Humane Animal Education & Services (HAES)

AKC CGC Evaluator

Assistance Dog Team Advocate

The American Red Cross (Volunteer/Emergency Shelter)

Putnam County Emergency Animal Support Team, Staff

Putnam County Pet-Friendly Evacuation Shelter Team,

County Coordinator

Member of Service Dog Central, Moderator of Forum

Member and Moderator of large German Shepherd Dog Forum Public Safety Instructor, Fire & Life Safety Classes for Children

Past Volunteer Work

First Responder with West Putnam Volunteer Fire Department

Board of Directors, West Putnam Volunteer Fire Department

Board of Directors, The Humane Society of Northeast FL, Inc.

Retired from

Alachua County Sheriff's Office (FL), Dept. of the Jail Criminal Justice Technician II


For more info:

Service Dog Central Website & Forum

www.servicedogcentral.org

Assistance Dog Advocacy Project Blog

blog.workndog.org/adap/

Theresa can be reached at adap@karlskidsprogram.com

## Section 11

Training information and forms, brought to you by Victoria Warfel and Dream Dogz Behavior Center.

Arrow

## Physician Form

In my professional opinion,

_____

is disabled and would benefit from having a service/
assistance dog.

Doctor name _____

_____

Address _____

Phone _____

Signature _____

Date _____

## Veterinarian Form

I have examined _____,
owned by _____.

This dog appears to be healthy, parasite-free, and current on vaccinations.

Vaccination dates:

Exam _____

Rabies _____

Distemper _____

Parvo _____

Bordetella _____

Fecal _____

Heartworm _____

Flea Prevention _____

This dog does not appear to have any training or behavior issues that would interfere with working as a Service Dog.

Veterinarian _____
Address _____
Phone _____

Signature_____

Date _____

## Service Dog Candidate

___ House training (potty on cue)

___ Socialize your dog to everyone—kids, strollers, bicycles, skate boards, joggers, wheelchairs, walkers, etc. A great place to do this is the city park. Sit on a bench with your dog and see how he reacts to the passers-by. You may be able to take your dog to local farmer's markets and fairs. Moving on to pet stores, feed stores, pet-friendly restaurants, and home improvement stores, as allowed.

___ Habituate your dog to his environment—television, vacuum cleaner, doorbell, lawnmower, etc.

___ Puppy socialization class

___ Basic Obedience

___ Intermediate Obedience

___ Advanced Obedience

___ AKC Canine Good Citizen Prep course

___ AKC Canine Good Citizen Test

___ At least 1 year old

## Service Dog In Training

___ Continue with Obedience training, as needed

___ Task training

___ Public access field trips (at least 30 hours)

___ Minimum 6 months of training and SD Evaluation

___ Document your training classes and training homework. You should log at least 120 hours of training time.

___ At least 30 hours should be field trip/public access outings.

___ Dog must be able to perform sit, down, come, stay, heel off-leash.

___ Absolutely NO dog or person aggression. No biting, snapping, snarling, growling, lunging, or barking.

___ No begging for food or for petting while on duty.

___ Ignores food dropped nearby.

___ No sniffing merchandise or people while on duty.

___ No potty accidents while in public.

| Dog Name: | |
|---|---|
| Breed: | |
| Microchip # | |
| AKC ID # | |
| County Lic # | |
| Handler Name: | |
| Address: | |
| City, State, Zip: | |
| Phone # | |
| Email: | |

## Task Training

Goal: _____

Steps to reach goal:

1._____

2._____

3._____

4._____

5._____

Notes:_____

_____

_____

_____

_____

## Task Training

Goal: _____

Steps to reach goal:

1._____

2._____

3._____

4._____

5._____

Notes:_____

_____

_____

_____

_____

## Task Training

Goal: _____

Steps to reach goal:

1._____

2._____

3._____

4._____

5._____


Notes:_____

_____

_____

_____

_____

## Task Training

Goal: _____

Steps to reach goal:

1._____

2._____

3._____

4._____

5._____

Notes:_____

_____

_____

_____

_____

## Task Training

Goal: _____

Steps to reach goal:

1._____

2._____

3._____

4._____

5._____


Notes:_____

_____

_____

_____

_____

| | | | | Hours Total: | |
|------|------|----------|--------|---|-------|
| Date | Time | Location | Skills | | Hours |
| | | | | | |
| | | | | | |
| | | | | | |
| | | | | | |
| | | | | | |
| | | | | | |
| | | | | | |
| | | | | | |
| | | | | | |
| | | | | Hours Total: | |

267

| | | | | Hours Total: | |
|---|---|---|---|---|---|
| Date | Time | Location | Skills | | Hours |
| | | | | | |
| | | | | | |
| | | | | | |
| | | | | | |
| | | | | | |
| | | | | | |
| | | | | | |
| | | | | | |
| | | | | | |
| | | | | Hours Total: | |

| | | | | Hours Total: | |
|---|---|---|---|---|---|
| Date | Time | Location | Skills | | Hours |
| | | | | | |
| | | | | | |
| | | | | | |
| | | | | | |
| | | | | | |
| | | | | | |
| | | | | | |
| | | | | | |
| | | | | | |
| | | | | Hours Total: | |

269

| | | | Hours Total: | |
|---|---|---|---|---|
| Date | Time | Location | Skills | Hours |
| | | | | |
| | | | | |
| | | | | |
| | | | | |
| | | | | |
| | | | | |
| | | | | |
| | | | | |
| | | | | |
| | | | Hours Total: | |

| | | | | Hours Total: | |
|---|---|---|---|---|---|
| Date | Time | Location | Skills | | Hours |
| | | | | | |
| | | | | | |
| | | | | | |
| | | | | | |
| | | | | | |
| | | | | | |
| | | | | | |
| | | | | | |
| | | | | | |
| | | | | Hours Total: | |

271

| | | | | Hours Total: | |
|---|---|---|---|---|---|
| Date | Time | Location | Skills | | Hours |
| | | | | | |
| | | | | | |
| | | | | | |
| | | | | | |
| | | | | | |
| | | | | | |
| | | | | | |
| | | | | | |
| | | | | Hours Total: | |

272

| | | | | Hours Total: | |
|------|------|----------|--------|---|---|
| Date | Time | Location | Skills | | Hours |
| | | | | | |
| | | | | | |
| | | | | | |
| | | | | | |
| | | | | | |
| | | | | | |
| | | | | | |
| | | | | | |
| | | | | | |
| | | | | Hours Total: | |

| | | | | Hours Total: | |
|---|---|---|---|---|---|
| Date | Time | Location | Skills | | Hours |
| | | | | | |
| | | | | | |
| | | | | | |
| | | | | | |
| | | | | | |
| | | | | | |
| | | | | | |
| | | | | | |
| | | | | | |
| | | | | Hours Total: | |

| | | | | Hours Total: | |
|---|---|---|---|---|---|
| Date | Time | Location | Skills | | Hours |
| | | | | | |
| | | | | | |
| | | | | | |
| | | | | | |
| | | | | | |
| | | | | | |
| | | | | | |
| | | | | | |
| | | | | | |
| | | | | Hours Total: | |

275

| | | | | Hours Total: | |
|---|---|---|---|---|---|
| Date | Time | Location | Skills | | Hours |
| | | | | | |
| | | | | | |
| | | | | | |
| | | | | | |
| | | | | | |
| | | | | | |
| | | | | | |
| | | | | | |
| | | | | | |
| | | | | Hours Total: | |

Notes:_____

_____

_____

_____

_____

_____

_____

_____

_____

_____

_____

Notes:_____

_____

_____

_____

_____

_____

_____

_____

_____

_____

_____

_____

Notes:_____

_____

_____

_____

_____

_____

_____

_____

_____

_____

_____

_____

_____

Notes:_____

_____

_____

_____

_____

_____

_____

_____

_____

_____

_____

_____

Notes:_____

_____

_____

_____

_____

_____

_____

_____

_____

_____

_____

## Dream Dogz Blog - Arrow on a Plane

Arrow has flown with us to Washington, DC for the International Association of Canine Professionals annual conference, and with me to Portland, Maine for Kayce Cover's Perception Modification certification camp. He flies with me later this month when I go to Birmingham, Alabama to visit with Rick Clark at The Barking Zone.

As my Service Dog, Arrow flies in the cabin with me. After I make the reservations online, and choose my aisle seat just behind the wings, I call the airline to inform them that I will be traveling with my service dog.

When we arrive at the airport, he rides the parking lot shuttle to the terminal. He has one last potty break, and we check any bags. We proceed thru security, usually the guards will wave us to the front of the line. After I show my identification, and load up the bins to be x-ray scanned, a guard will direct us to the metal detector line. Arrow sits on one side while I go through, once I clear the metal detector, I call him though to me. Sometimes, we take off his vest and send that through, other times he can wear it. It is easiest to go through with a slip lead on him. One time when we went through, they sent his vest, collar and leash through the x-ray scanner, so he ended up doing a down-stay in the middle of a crowded airport with people everywhere, with absolutely nothing on.

We wait at the gate and board when they call for people who need extra assistance. I stow any carry on luggage above my head and Arrow curls up at my feet. Some people fly with their service dog in the very first row, but I find Arrow has more room when he can tuck under the row in front of us. He has not been bothered by take off, landing, or turbulence. He usually sleeps right through it. When I flew with my family, I handed his leash to them when I used the restroom. When I fly on my own, Arrow comes into the restroom with me. It's a bit awkward, but life is nothing if it isn't an adventure!

Arrow is on Wendy Volhard's Natural diet, so I pack his cereal bars and supplements, and when we land, I buy ground beef and yogurt for him. I pack different collars and leashes, along with a toy, food and water bowls. Arrow is brushed and his nails are dremmeled before we leave.

If we are getting a rental car, I let them know I am traveling with my service dog. I will also bring a sheet for him to lay on while in the car. I inform the hotel, and usually ask for a first

floor room. I bring plenty of poo bags to clean up after him, and will buy a roll of paper towels in case we need them.

Traveling with your service dog requires more planning than traveling on your own. Here are our **tips on flying with your service dog**:

1. Give yourself extra time. You don't want to have to rush, you want to have plenty of time so you can relax and explain everything to your dog. I tell Arrow exactly what is going to happen, "Arrow, we are going on a plane, it's like a really big car that goes up in the sky."

2. Plan. For everything. Check at the airport to locate where the service dog potty areas are. Have a packing list so you don't forget anything. Pack more than you think you will need, and if you forget, hopefully you can buy it when you land. Depending on how long you will be gone, you can order food from Amazon.com and have it sent to where you are going.

3. Get extra rest. Travel can be tiring, for both you and for your service dog. Make sure you exercise your dog ahead of time.

http://www.dreamk9.com/2014/11/arrow-on-a-plane/

## Dream Dogz Blog - Arrow Visits Disney World

Arrow visited Disney World this past weekend. We have gone before, but this was his very first visit. As my service dog, Arrow can accompany me. He has flown with me to Maine and to Washington DC, curled up under the seat where you stow your carry on. However, he never experienced DISNEY. The crowds, sights, smells, rides, characters, distractions, did I mention crowds? Let me tell you about his adventure.

First, Arrow was amazing! We visited Epcot the first day, Animal Kingdom the second day and Magic Kingdom the third day. After a day of walking the park, when we got back to the hotel, Arrow wanted to play! We played hide the toy, and he found it every time.

At Epcot, Arrow's very first ride was the tram from the parking lot. He also rode Ellen's Energy Adventure and Spaceship Earth. We walked the World Showcase and saw Reflections of China. Since the International Food and Wine Festival was going on, it was more crowded than we have seen before. Arrow ignored the people, and the food.

Ellen's Energy Adventure was easy for him. He napped during most of it, and didn't even notice the dinosaurs. Spaceship Earth was a little different. We used the mobility entrance, where we were met by cast members who stopped the ride for him to get on. We always used the mobility entrance when the ride had one. Rich and Luc sat in the front of the car, and Arrow and I sat in the rear. He watched history unfold, and looked from side to side. There are some steep inclines, but I had hold of him, and he leaned against me. It was his first big ride, and he enjoyed it.

At Animal Kingdom, Arrow met Mickey & Minnie, saw the Festival of the Lion King and Flights of Wonder, went on

Kilimanjaro Safari, and watched Luc and Rich win at Fossil Fun Games. On Safari, Arrow had to be tethered to the vehicle, and remain in a down/stay. Even though he smelled the wild animals, he relaxed and slept for most of the ride. We noticed a pattern, Arrow can catch a nap whenever possible.

At Magic Kingdom, we took the Ferryboat over and the Monorail back to the parking lot. We started with one of my favorites, Haunted Mansion. We also rode Liberty Square Riverboat, "it's a small world,"  The Many Adventures of Winnie the Pooh, and Jungle Cruise. We watched the Festival of Fantasy Parade at Pecos Bill Tall Tale Inn and Cafe. The only ride we did that Arrow couldn't go on was Peter Pan's Flight. I hadn't done that before, so Luc and I did that, while Rich and Arrow waited.

Arrow enjoyed seeing the ghosts in Haunted Mansion. When we got the graveyard part, he lay down and napped. He and I rode together, and met Rich and Luc at the exit. On "it's a small world," we got our own boat to ride on. Guess what Arrow did during that ride? If you guessed he fell asleep, you are right!

Of course, people noticed Arrow and commented on him. Rich and Luc talked to lots of people about Arrow, told them that he is a medical alert service dog, and he is a Belgian Shepherd. Most of the parents would let their children know that he is a service dog, and they cannot say hello, which was greatly appreciated. Some kids ran up to us before their parents stopped them. Some kids tried to sneak pets as they were walking by. However, most of the people were terrific!

The cast members couldn't have been better. They asked if he would like some water, guided us to our seats, showed us where we should go, and chatted with us. We highly recommend Disney World, and will be visiting again soon!

## Arrow's Tips for Disney World with your Service Dog:

1. Pick up a Guide for Guests with Disabilities. There is a section for Service Animals, including ride restrictions and relief areas.

2. Have a rock-solid down/stay. Most every ride requested Arrow be in a down during the ride.

3. Train your dog to heel on both sides. There were times we needed Arrow to be on either side due to crowds.

4. Disney is the most magical place on earth, and is different from anything your dog has experienced before. Your dog must have patience and tolerate a lot. People snuck in pets when we walked by. People stared. We made sure we intercepted everything we could, and kept him blocked from crowds, but there were just so many people.

5. Be prepared. We were at the parks for 5-7 hours each day. We fed him before we left for the day and when we returned to the hotel. We brought a collapsable water bowl or asked for a bowl from one of the food vendors. We brought clean up bags. Arrow had plenty of nap time as well.

http://www.dreamk9.com/2014/10/arrow-visits-disney-world/

## Victoria Warfel

Owner and Head Trainer of Dream Dogz, LLC.

Victoria is the head trainer at Dream Dogz. She has been training in the Gainesville area since she moved there in 2005 with her family and her self-trained service dog, Boo. Victoria started as a food-based trainer, but realized the limitations and kept searching for a better way. After studying and combining many styles of training, she has developed her own training methods. She quickly became the go-to trainer for dogs with behavior issues. She opened Dream Dogz Training & Behavior Center in 2011. Before then, she was one of the trainers at Dogwood Park, trained in city parks, and in private homes.

Victoria is:

- a Certified Dog Trainer (IACP-CDT) and Professional Member of the International Association of Canine Professionals

- Perception Modification 1 Certified in the Syn Alia Training System

- an AKC-Approved Canine Good Citizen Evaluator, Community Canine Evaluator, Urban Canine Good Citizen Evaluator, S.T.A.R. Puppy Instructor & Evaluator, thru the American Kennel Club

- a Certified Trick Dog Instructor (CTDI), awarded Trainer of the Year from Do More With Your Dog!

- Founder of the Freedom, Remote Collar Training Method

- a volunteer with Karl's Kids Program - Alachua County Project Coordinator

- voted 2013, 2014, & 2015 Best of Gainesville for Dog Training

## Appendix A -- Acronyms

AAA -- Animal Assisted Activities

AAD -- Allergy Alert Dog

AAT -- Animal Assisted Therapy

ACAA -- Air Carriers Access Act

ADA -- Americans with Disabilities Act

ADAAA -- ADA Amendments Act

ADAP -- Assistance Dog Advocacy Project (Project of Karl's Kids Program, Inc.)

ADI -- Assistance Dogs International, Inc.

AKC -- American Kennel Club

ATTS -- American Temperament Test Society, Inc. (A nationally known organization)

BAT -- Behavior Adjustment Training (For fear, frustration, and aggression in dogs)

BSL -- Breed Specific Legislation

CFR -- Codes of Federal Regulation

CGC -- Canine Good Citizen Certificate or Title

CGCA -- Canine Good Citizen Title Advanced

DAD -- Diabetic Alert Dog

DHS -- Department of Human Services

292

DOJ -- Department of Justice

DPT -- Deep Pressure Therapy

EEOC -- Equal Employment Opportunity Commission (Title I Regulatory Agency)

ESA/ESD -- Emotional Support Animal, Emotional Support Dog

FHAct -- Fair Housing Act

FR -- The Federal Register

GPO -- U.S. Government Printing Office

HoH -- Hard of Hearing

HUD -- Housing and Urban Development

IAADP -- International Association of Assistance Dog Partners

IDEA -- Individuals with Disabilities Education Act

KsKs -- Karl's Kids Program, Inc.

NPRM -- Notice of Proposed Rulemaking

OFR -- The Office of the Federal Register

OT -- Owner Trained

PA -- Public Access

PAT -- Public Access Test

PSD -- Psychiatric Service Dog

PSDIT -- Psychiatric Service Dog-In-Training

PTSD -- Post Traumatic Stress Disorder

PWD -- Person with a disability

SCOTUS -- The Supreme Court of the United States

SD -- Service Dog

SDC -- Service Dog Central

SDIT -- Service Dog-In-Training

TBI -- Traumatic Brain Injury

TD -- Therapy Dog

TT -- Temperament Tested (Title for dogs given by the ATTS)

VHA -- Veterans Health Administration

Boo

## Appendix B -- Definitions

**Access Board**: The Architectural and Transportation Barriers Compliance Board, an independent federal agency devoted to accessibility for people with disabilities.

**Accessible:** Accessibility. Addresses buildings and the like, a site, facility, work environment, service, or program that is easy to approach, enter, operate, participate in, and/or use safely and with dignity by a person with a disability.

**Americans with Disabilities Act (ADA):** a comprehensive, federal civil rights law that prohibits discrimination on the basis of disabilities in employment, state and local government programs and activities, public accommodations, transportation, and telecommunications.

**Americans with Disabilities Act Amendments Act (ADAAA):** enacted on September 25, 2008, and becoming effective on January 1, 2009, making a number of significant changes to the definition of "disability" and directing the U.S. Equal Employment Opportunity Commission (EEOC) to amend its ADA regulations to reflect the changes made by the ADAAA. The final regulations were published in the Federal Register on March 25, 2011.

**AKC:** The American Kennel Club. Registration in this organization does not show dog's status as suitable for breeding or that the dog is a fair to good representative of the breed. The AKC is a dog registry and only shows that the dog's parents, grandparents and further back were included in a breed registry.

**ARC:** The American Red Cross. In their Mass Care Shelter Policy they allow handler's to bring their Assistance/Service Dogs based on DOJ Title II.

**Assistance Dog:** This term can be used in place of Service Dog. Some Federal Laws and some State Statutes will use one or the other while some go back and forth between the terms. Most laws in other countries use the term Assistance Dog.

**Auxiliary Aids and Services:** Aids and Services offered under titles II and III of the ADA, includes a wide range of services and devices that promote effective communication or allows access to goods and services.

**CGC:** The American Kennel Club's Canine Good Citizen Certificate or Title.

**CGCA:** The American Kennel Club's Canine Good Citizen Advanced Title more formally known as the AKC Community Canine Title.

**CGCU:** The American Kennel Club's Urban Canine Good Citizen Title.

**Covered Entity:** Per the ADA, "covered entity" is an entity that must comply with the law. Under title I, covered entities include employers, employment agencies, labor organizations, or joint labor-management committees. Under title II, covered entities include state and local government instrumentalities, the National Railroad Passenger Corporation, and other commuter authorities, and public transportation systems. Under title III, covered entities include public accommodations such as restaurants, hotels, grocery stores, retail stores, etc., as well as privately owned transportation systems.

**Department of Justice:** The DOJ is the Federal Regulatory Agency. It was placed over ADA Title II - State and Local Governments and Title III - Public Accomodations by Congress. It has sent out joint documents with other agencies such as HUD on various matters of public concern.

**Department of Transportation:** The DOT is a Federal Regulatory Agency. The Department of Transportation was established by an act of Congress on October 15, 1966. *The top priorities at DOT are to keep the traveling public safe and secure, increase their mobility, and have our transportation system contribute to the nation's economic growth.*

**Disability:** The term *disability* is more generally accepted over the older used term *handicap*.

**Dwelling:** Under the FHAct, *dwelling* means any building, structure, or portion thereof which is occupied as, or designed or intended for occupancy as, a residence by one or more families, and any vacant land which is offered for sale or lease for the construction or location thereon of any such building, structure, or portion thereof.

**Fair Housing Act:** The FHAct applies to both private and public housing.

**Family:** Under the FHAct, family includes a single individual.

**Federal Register:** The daily journal of the United State Government.

**Final Rules:** (Per the Federal Register) This category contains regulations that apply to the general public and have final legal effect. It also includes interim final rules, direct final rules, and various determinations, interpretive rules, and policy statements. The documents cite to the Code of Federal Regulations, which contains the codified text of final rules, and is published annually in 50 titles.

**Handicap:** The term *handicap* is contained in the Fair Housing Amendments Act of 1988. Under the Fair Housing Act, *handicap* and *disability* have the same legal meaning though newer documents use the term *disability*.

**Impairment:** A term used in the ADA definition of disability. Includes any physiological disorder or condition, cosmetic disfigurement, or anatomical loss affecting one or more body systems, such as neurological, musculoskeletal, special sense organs, respiratory (including speech organs), cardiovascular, reproductive, digestive, genitourinary, immune, circulatory, hemic, lymphatic, skin, and endocrine; or any mental or psychological disorder, such as an intellectual disability (formerly termed "mental retardation"), organic brain syndrome, emotional or mental illness, and specific learning disabilities.

**Nexus:** A legal relationship

**The Office of the Federal Register:** The OFR provides access to the official text of Federal Laws,

Presidential Documents, Administrative Regulations and Notices, Descriptions of Federal Organizations, and Programs and Activities.

**Person**: Under the FHAct, *person* includes one or more individuals, corporations, partnerships, associations, labor organizations, legal representatives, mutual companies, joint-stock companies, trusts, unincorporated organizations, trustees, trustees in cases under title 11 [of the United States Code], receivers, and fiduciaries.

**Prevailing Law:** Along with Federal laws, state and local laws may also address benefits to individuals with disabilities. The law with the superior force, that is giving the most protections or benefits will prevail. Federal laws are considered the base or minimum level of protections and benefits.

**Proposed Rules:** (Per the Federal Register) These documents announce and explain agencies' plans to solve problems and accomplish goals, and give interested persons an opportunity to submit comments to improve the final regulation. It also includes advance notices of proposed rulemaking, petitions for rulemaking, negotiated rulemakings, and various proposed determinations and interpretations.

**Public Accommodations:** Entities that must comply with Title III. The term includes facilities whose operations affect commerce and fall within at least one of the following 12 categories: places of lodging (e.g., inns, hotels, motels) (except for owner-occupied establishments renting fewer than six rooms); establishments serving food or drink (e.g., restaurants and bars); places of exhibition or entertainment (e.g., motion picture houses, theaters, concert halls, stadiums); places of public gathering (e.g., auditoriums, convention centers, lecture halls); sales or rental establishments (e.g., bakeries, grocery stores, hardware stores, shopping centers); service establishments (e.g., laundromats, dry-cleaners, banks, barber shops, beauty shops, travel services, shoe repair services, funeral parlors, gas stations, offices of accountants or lawyers, pharmacies, insurance offices, professional offices of health care providers, hospitals); public transportation terminals, depots, or stations (not including facilities relating to air transportation); places of public display or collection (e.g., museums, libraries, galleries); places of recreation (e.g., parks, zoos, amusement parks); places of education (e.g., nursery schools, elementary, secondary, undergraduate, or postgraduate private schools); social service center establishments (e.g., day care centers, senior citizen centers, homeless shelters, food banks, adoption agencies); and places of exercise or recreation (e.g., gymnasiums, health spas, bowling alleys, golf courses).

301

**Public Entity:** Entities that must comply with Title II. The term is defined as: any state or local government; any department, agency, special purpose district, or other instrumentality of a state or local government; or certain commuter authorities as well as AMTRAK. It does not include the federal government.

**Reasonable Accommodation:** Under the Fair Housing Act, a *reasonable accommodation* is a change, exception, or adjustment to a rule, policy, practice, or service.

**Reasonable Modification:** Under the Fair Housing Act, a *reasonable modification* is a structural change made to the premises.

**Section 504 of the Rehabilitation Act of 1973 (Section 504):** Section 504 is a federal law designed to protect the rights of individuals with disabilities in programs and activities that receive Federal financial assistance.

**Service Animal:**
Per the ARC -- Follows DOJ standards for Title II.

Per the DOJ -- *Service animal means any dog that is individually trained to do work or perform tasks for the benefit of an individual with a disability, including a physical, sensory, psychiatric, intellectual, or other mental*

302

disability. Other species of animals, whether wild or domestic, trained or untrained, are not service animals for the purposes of this definition. The work or tasks performed by a service animal must be directly related to the individual's disability. Examples of work or tasks include, but are not limited to, assisting individuals who are blind or have low vision with navigation and other tasks, alerting individuals who are deaf or hard of hearing to the presence of people or sounds, providing non-violent protection or rescue work, pulling a wheelchair, assisting an individual during a seizure, alerting individuals to the presence of allergens, retrieving items such as medicine or the telephone, providing physical support and assistance with balance and stability to individuals with mobility disabilities, and helping persons with psychiatric and neurological disabilities by preventing or interrupting impulsive or destructive behaviors. The crime deterrent effects of an animal's presence and the provision of emotional support, well-being, comfort, or companionship do not constitute work or tasks for the purposes of this definition.

Per DOT / ACAA -- The Air Carrier Access Act. § 382.55 Miscellaneous provisions.

(a) Carriers shall permit dogs and other service animals used by persons with a disability to accompany the persons on a flight.

*(1) Carriers shall accept as evidence that an animal is a service animal identification cards, other written documentation, presence of harnesses or markings on harnesses, tags, or the credible verbal assurances of the qualified individual with a disability using the animal.*

Per HUD *-- ... in the case of assistance/service animals, an individual with a disability must demonstrate a nexus between his or her disability and the function the service animal provides. The Department's position has been that animals necessary as a reasonable accommodation do not necessarily need to have specialized training. Some animals perform tasks that require training, and others provide assistance that does not require training.*

## Index

3 - Disclaimer & Dedication

5 - Introduction

6 - Section I

7 - Some Things to Consider for Owner Training

9 - There are Three Parts to Training a SD

10 - Obedience

11 - Public Access Work

12 - Public Access Testing

12 - Assistance Dog International (ADI) Public Access Test

13 - International Association of Assistance Dog Partners (IAADP) on ADI's Testing

15 - Task Training

16 - Logs

16 - Training & Medical Records Log

19 - Dogs for Service Work

23 - Size of Service Dogs

26 - Tasks

28 - Strong Tasks and Weak Tasks

29 - How Many Tasks Are Required

31 - Doing Work or Performing Tasks

36 - Definitions of Tasks from the Federal Register

38 - Nondiscrimination on the Basis of Disability by Public Accommodations and in Commercial Facilities

44 - Stages in the Life Cycles of an Assistance/Service Dog

46 - Assistance/Service Dog Candidates

48 - Assistance/Service Dogs in Training

52 - Types of Laws

53 - Federal Laws

55 - Service Animals per the Department of Justice: Americans with Disabilities Act Title II Primer

59 - Service Animals ADA Requirements

66 - Frequently Asked Questions About Service Animals and the ADA

85 - Health Care Facilities, Guidelines for Environmental Infection Control in Health-Care Facilities

92 - Housing, Service Animal or Emotional Support Animal - Dog or Other in Housing Issues

94 - Reasonable Accommodations Under the Fair Housing Act

102 - Insurance Policy Restrictions as a Defense for Refusals to Make a Reasonable Accommodation

105 - Department of Housing and Urban Development: Pet Ownership for the Elderly and Persons with Disabilities

109 - Service Animals and Assistance Animals for People with Disabilities in Housing and HUD-Funded Programs

114 - Travel, The Air Carrier Access Act

117 - Guidance Concerning Service Animals: Nondiscrimination on the Basis of Disability in Air Travel

129 - TSA Cares

132 - Answers to Frequently Asked Questions Concerning Air Travel of People with Disabilities

148 - Amtrak

150 - Taxicabs, Shuttles and Limousine Services

151 - Accessible Lodging

153 - Department of the Interior - National Parks Service

154 - Section 504 of the Rehab Act

155 - U.S. Postal Services (USPS)

157 - The ADA of 1990 and ADAAA of 2008

158 - Title I (Employment)

160 - Title II (Public Entities)

193- Title III (Public Accommodations)

200 - Inquiries, Exclusions, Charges, and Other Specific Rules Related to Service Animals

203 - Minimal Protection Change to Non-Violent Protection

207 - Other Federal Agencies with ADA Responsibilities

209 - Helpful Contact Info

212 - Employment

216 - Job Accommodation Network (JAN)

218 - Internal Revenue Service (IRS)

219 - Florida State Information

221 - Florida State Statutes

221 - During Disasters and Emergencies

221 - Registry of Persons with Special Needs

223 - Traffic Regulations to Assist Mobility-Impaired Persons

223 - Rights of an Individual with a Disability; Use of a Service Animal; Discrimination in Prohibited discrimination in Public Employment, Public

Accommodations, and Housing Accommodations;
Penalties

232 - Lodging and Food

240 - Bite by a Police or Service Dog; Exemption from
Quarantine

243 - Service Dogs in Florida Schools

248 - Therapy Dog

250 - Emotional Support Dog (Animal)

251 - Position on Breed Bans

254 - Theresa A. Jennings


256 - Section II

257 - Physician Form

258 - Veterinarian Form

259 - Service Dog Candidate

260 - Service Dog In Training

261 - Dog Information

262 - Task Training

267 - Training Log

277 - Notes

282 - Dream Dogz Blog - Arrow on a Plane

285 - Dream Dogz Blog - Arrow Visits Disney World

290 - Victoria Warfel

292 - Appendix A -- Acronyms

295 - Appendix B -- Definitions

305 - Index

CPSIA information can be obtained at www.ICGtesting.com
Printed in the USA
LVOW04s1948030915

452717LV00030B/1232/P